I took Gene's class on "Completing That Book." It was just what I needed. How does an engineer, steeped in mathematics and science, convert a vivid dream into a novel? Gene has the answer. His focus on planning and structure appealed to my background and the way I like to work, but still left lots of room to explore my creative side—and my story. Gene provided a step-by-step method that develops my ideas and keeps me motivated. His approach can be applied to both nonfiction and fiction. With his help, I am well on my way.

—*Jonathan Hops*

Gene Perret makes something difficult, like getting published, seem easy and possible. His course titled, "Finishing that Book You've Always Wanted to Write" will make my name a household word. Thanks to Gene, I can finally become famous. Now I can paper my bathroom in the large house I will buy with my earnings with the rejections letters from the past. Thanks Gene, you are my inspiration and the best teacher ever!!!

—*Marcia Hinds*

For the past decade, I have been planning to write my book. Gene's class gave me the framework to get it started and organized. His encouragement and experience in the "business" has been invaluable.

—*Jeanne Howard*

I enjoyed Gene's style of teaching; his humorous approach to writing made going to class quite entertaining. And the organizational tips helped me get on the right track for starting my book. Having the steps outlined one by one made the daunting task of writing a nonfiction book a little less intimidating.

—*Jodai Saremi*

I found Gene Perret's class to be inspiring and captivating with real life stories of his work in show business with Carol Burnett, Jim Nabors, and especially my favorite, Bob Hope. Using real life stories, along with supplying the various techniques to follow while planning/writing will certainly help me as I move forward with my latest book. Thank you VERY much.

—*Linda Scott*

Prior to the class, I had a book in progress but after completing the outline and writing a draft of two of the chapters, I was "stuck" ... and I remained so for the next 12 plus months! That is until I took your writing class about how to finish and market my book.

The result of finishing your class is that now I have a proven "pathway" to follow, prepared by an accomplished author of over 40 books and taught by a very interesting teacher.

With this new "pathway" to follow, I now know what I need to do to finish my book, how to do it, how to use a proven organizational method, how to schedule my writing and tailor it to my lifestyle, how to find and meet publishers, and much more.

—*Nancy S. Altman*

I attended Gene's writing class and found that his years of successful experience writing about and for the entertainment industry brought a unique and insightful view of not only the art of writing a book, but about a man who loves his craft!

—*Linda Hertz*

I love having a road map when venturing into unknown territory, and Gene Perret's class provided a terrific step-by-step approach that anyone who needs help organizing and completing their book can follow. I highly recommend it!

—*Patricia Jones, MBA*

Gene Perret is not only a gifted writer, but a natural teacher. His gift of gab, along with his wit and humor while he imparts well thought out information in a patient, unpretentious manner, make his classes a delight.

—*Diane du Bois*

For anyone who has ever considered or tried writing a book, Gene provides the practical tools and expert guidance necessary to not only complete your book but to complete a good book. The sooner you read Gene's book, the sooner you will be on the bookshelf.

—*Sophia Fischer*

Write Your Book
Now!

A proven system to start and FINISH the book you've always wanted to write!

Gene Perret

Quill Driver Books
Fresno, California

Write Your Book *NOW!*
A proven system to start and FINISH
the book you've always wanted to write.
© 2011 Gene Perret. All rights reserved.

Published by Quill Driver Books,
an imprint of Linden Publishing.
2006 S. Mary, Fresno, California, 93721
559-233-6633 / 800-345-4447
QuillDriverBooks.com

Quill Driver Books is a trademark of Linden Publishing, Inc.

ISBN: 978-1-61035-006-8
135798642

Printed in the USA on acid-free paper.

Library of Congress Cataloging-in-Publication Data

Perret, Gene.
  Write your book now! : a proven system to start and FINISH the book you've
always wanted to write. / Gene Perret.
      p. cm.
  Includes index.
  ISBN 978-1-61035-006-8 (pbk. : acid-free paper)
  1. Authorship. I. Title.
  PN145.P434 2011
  808'.02--dc23
                                          2011016392

For Joe

CONTENTS

WHAT THIS BOOK IS AND IS NOT

LIKE MOST BOOK BUYERS AND READERS, you've probably already glanced at the front cover of this book. More than likely, you've also flipped it over and read some or all of the text on the back cover. That back cover is tremendously important. It's significant not so much for whatever images may be displayed on it or for the copy that it contains, but simply because it's there. It exists. The back cover indicates that the book is finished. It's done. It's complete. You can't put a back cover on a book that is incomplete.

The back cover tells you that there are no more manuscript pages due for the book. Everything the author had to say, wanted to say, and did say is compressed between the front and the back covers of this book. It has all been written, edited, typeset, printed and published.

Once that back cover is affixed to the rest of the book, there's no way the author can beg for an extension of the deadline. No publisher would listen if the author said, "I've got the book started and it's going pretty well, but I want to take a short break from it. Why don't you put a front and back cover on it and get it to the bookstores? I'll get around to finishing it when I feel more inspired."

No. Once the book—any book—is printed and the back cover is attached, that book is done.

That's the purpose of *this* particular volume—to get you, your writing, and your entire project to the back cover, figuratively and literally. My book will encourage and inspire you to get started on that book you've always wanted to write. More important, it will help you *finish* your book. My program will carefully guide you step-by-step through the processes required to organize your thoughts, plan your book, prepare a writing schedule, do a little advance marketing, and edit and rewrite your manuscript in order to self-publish it or send it to a publisher.

That's what this book is: a field-tested game plan, providing strategy and precise tactics to help you to write the book that you've been carrying around in your soul.

This is not an instructional book on the craft of writing. Reading this volume will not help you create captivating story lines or develop strong and consistent characters. The lessons in this book are not aimed at building your vocabulary or employing proper sentence structure. It's not interested in improving your writing style or technique. It doesn't even care if you spell correctly.

Those are all valuable writing tools, of course, and you should take them seriously. However, my book, and the program it offers, is exclusively devoted to one goal—to get you to *finish* your book. The most graceful, expressive, coherent writing in the world is useless if it's left unfinished.

Suppose for a moment that Charles Dickens had written, "It was the best of times, it was the worst of times," and then showed it to his Aunt Martha who said, "I don't know what you're talking about, Charlie. If it's the best of times, it can't be the worst of times and if it's the worst of times, it can't be the best of times. Honestly, I think you should spend more time writing things that people can understand rather than this jibber-jabber that makes no sense at all." Dickens could have thought to himself, *you know my Aunt Martha's generally right. Maybe that opening sentence was a bit ambiguous. You know what? I'll just postpone writing* A Tale of Two Cities *until I can come up with a better opening—maybe in a couple of months or so.*

What good would his glorious writing have been if Dickens never finished the book?

Starting and completing your book is vastly more satisfying than writing a brilliant, poetic, captivating two or three chapters…and then nothing more. So, rather than de-emphasizing scintillating prose, my book is actually promoting it by giving would-be authors the tools they need to finish their books so the rest of the world can enjoy their brilliance!

THIS IS *YOUR* BOOK

The book you want to write is *your* book. It's an idea that you've carried within yourself for some time now, perhaps for many years. It's something that you want or need (perhaps very deeply) to say. Your book deserves to be born. So grant yourself permission right now to start, write, and complete *your* book.

There are no prerequisites to writing the book you want to write. You don't have to pass a test and be certified as you would to practice law, medicine, or even to drive a car. The only qualification is that you want to write it. That's enough.

I will offer suggestions to guide you during the process, but you, the writer, should always remain true to your idea, your concept, your book.

"THE WRITE YOUR BOOK *NOW!*" SYSTEM

If you've been trying to write a book and you've had trouble getting the task done, this book offers a writer-tested system you can turn to. This program will help you prepare and organize the elements of your book. It will teach you how to plan a workable writing schedule, guide you through the chapter-by-chapter writing process, and assist you in rewriting and preparing your manuscript for publication. This process will be a powerful ally in helping you complete your book.

I know the system works because I have used it to publish many books. I've also taught classes based on this system. Many of my students have found it to be the element that inspired them to channel their efforts into finally finishing books they had been working on but not completing. These students have often provided me with valuable feedback that I've integrated into the program, strengthening it further.

One thing I always mention to the students in my eight-week classes is that they should recognize that writing a book takes time. None of them will start and finish a book within the eight weeks of scheduled classes. The same advice applies to you, also. It will take time to finish your book—much more time than it takes to read this volume. Therefore, I recommend that you read through this text first to acquaint yourself with the principles of my program. Then use it as a guide as you begin applying those principles to the starting, writing, and completing of your own book.

Remember that at the beginning of this Introduction I talked about looking at the cover of the book, then flipping it over and examining the back cover? Soon, you'll be able to do that with your own book. You'll discover it's a great feeling.

CHAPTER 1

SO WHAT'S KEEPING YOU FROM WRITING YOUR BOOK?

YOU HAVE A BOOK YOU WANT TO WRITE. It's a good idea, it'll make a fine book, and you are a fine writer—but your book is not getting written. Why?

The answer to that question is critical to completing your book. Not finishing your book is not really the problem. It's merely the symptom. The reason why you're not completing your book is the problem.

If you go to your doctor and say, "Doc, I've got a tummy ache," the doctor is going to want to find out why you've got a pain in your stomach. He or she might prod you and poke you, maybe even send you for tests in order to answer the basic important question—why? What's causing the symptom? The doctor knows there could be any one of several possible reasons for the problem. Now the MD has to discover which specific reason is causing your specific pain. That information will tell him or her how to treat it. And, then your MD will know what medicine or procedure will make it go away.

Henny Youngman used to have a joke that said, "A guy went to the doctor and said, 'Doc, it hurts when I lift my arm.' The doctor said, 'Don't lift your arm.'" The solution was that simple.

That's an old gag, but sometimes the solution can be that simple. Find out the "why" and resolve it.

You're reading this volume because you have a book that you want to write, but you're having trouble getting it into manuscript form. That's the symptom. As a writer, that's your "tummy ache." Now, just like the physician, you must probe, prod, and uncover the cause.

There are many reasons why writers have difficulty completing a book. Often, simply finding the cause can be the solution. In other cases, definite steps must be taken to correct the problem. Let's look at some of these reasons why writers don't finish their manuscripts. With each cause we study, I'll also suggest solutions.

Of course, not all of the problems will apply to each reader. (Just as not all of the reasons for a "tummy ache" will be present in each patient.) It's up to you to read through the various reasons and isolate the ones that are influencing your writing (or lack of writing) and then take the steps to eliminate those problems.

Here are some of the reasons why you may be having trouble completing your book:

1. You Never Begin the Book

There's an old proverb that says, "The journey of one thousand miles begins with the first step." If you don't take the first step, you can't possibly take the final step that gets you to that thousandth mile. Similarly, if you don't begin your book, you can't finish your book. The only way to get to the last page of your manuscript, obviously, is to type the first page of the manuscript. Typing the first page, of course, doesn't guarantee that you'll complete your book, but it is unarguably a prerequisite.

If you investigate, you may find underlying reasons why you are reluctant to begin your book. One possibility is that you feel that you'll never be able to either get an agent or publishing firm interested in any book you write. It's not an unusual attitude. However, it's very much premature. It's also quite self-fulfilling. You convince yourself that your book will never sell; consequently, you don't write it; consequently, you don't sell it. The solution here is to simply ignore the possibility of a sale. "Ignore" may be too strong a word. How about postponing the idea of selling your book? Push that problem back until you come to it. The immediate problems are to start and complete your book. When that's done, you can begin the campaign to sell it.

My system will suggest ways of beginning to market your book while you're in the process of writing it. I'll discuss ways of sending out query letters or even book proposals before the book is completed. A great incentive to completing a book is to have a publishing contract in hand. Nevertheless, whatever steps I advise and you take in order to market your book should not detract from the main goal—to finish your manuscript!

Another reason why you may be hesitant to start writing your book is because you feel that you'll never be able to finish it. Writing a complete book is indeed a challenging task to undertake, and from the starting point, the finish line appears a long way off. You may convince yourself that you'll never complete a full-sized book, so what's the point in beginning it?

My response to this problem is to look back at some of the work you've already accomplished in your life. Whatever you do for a living presently, review it. Take a look at the body of work that you've accomplished. It's probably tremendous. It's probably such that if you took a look at it as if you were just beginning that work, you'd say to yourself that there's no way you could do it. And yet you have done it. Someone once asked Bob Hope what he would do differently if he had his life to live over again. Hope said, "If I had my life to live over again, I wouldn't have the time." That's pretty much true of most of us.

So yes, the completion of a manuscript when viewed from the first blank page seems to be a long way off. It is. But it's doable. Many others have done it, and you can, too.

I once resisted a request from a publisher to write a book. I had never written a book and felt I couldn't complete a manuscript of 60,000 or 70,000 words. But the publisher talked me into it and acted as my editor, guiding me through the writing process. I did complete the book and published it in 1980. Since then, I've published almost forty books. So I was wrong in feeling that I couldn't complete a book. If you feel that way now, you're probably wrong, too.

◆ ◆ ◆

Solution: The solution to the problem of not starting your book might seem to be simply that you must start it. That, though, may be unwise. Yes, at some point, you do have to start the book, but you must start it with the key to my writing program: proper preparation. Read on to point 2.

2. **Starting Your Book Without Proper Preparation**

If you're going to take a motor trip somewhere, you don't just start your car, back out of the garage, and begin driving. You must have some idea of where you're going, and at least a general notion of how to get there. It's the same with starting a book. Turning on the computer and typing chapter one may be counterproductive. Admittedly, it does get your book started, which as I've said, is the necessary first step. However, it may get you started in the wrong direction and slow up the rest of the process. In fact, getting off to a bad start might convince you to not complete the book at all.

Before you begin typing text, you should have a good idea of what your book is about. You should envision those people you're writing the book for. The chapters should be organized in your mind—in fact, they should be organized on paper.

Writing a book is not a small task, but it doesn't have to be overwhelming. One of the main points of my system is that you can only complete a book by breaking it into smaller segments (I'll elaborate on that in the following chapter). However, doing that requires an overall plan to guarantee that all the pieces eventually will fit. It's like constructing a home. The contractor works on various facets of the building at any given time, yet he constantly refers to the blueprints. No contractor would start any portion of the building without first having a complete set of plans.

◆ ◆ ◆

Solution: In this book, I devote at least six chapters to planning your writing. There are suggestions on defining your book, organizing your thoughts, planning what you want to say, laying out the chapters, refining those chapters, and documenting your writing schedule.

Complete your reading of this book, and then follow the suggestions in order to not only get your book started, but get it started effectively. Yes, do take that proverbial first step on your thousand-mile journey, but be sure to begin it in the right direction. If you don't, you'll wind up having to make a journey of one thousand miles *and two steps*.

3. Not Having a Book in the First Place

For years I had a cartoon from the Sunday papers framed and hanging over my desk—directly over the computer monitor, in fact. It was there in plain view as a constant admonition. The cartoon featured an owl in a tree who sat at a typewriter ready to begin a great work of literature. In the first panel, the thought cloud over his head was blank. In the second panel, the thought cloud over his head remained blank. This continued for the first five panels, as the crumpled up discards grew larger and larger around his wastebasket. Finally...in the sixth panel, the thought panel over his head showed a brilliantly illustrated letter "A"—the kind you would see as the first letter in an ornately hand-lettered book. Then in the next panel, the owl/writer tapped his keyboard and it produced an ordinary, simple type-written letter "A." In the final panel, the thought cloud over the owl's head was blank again.

The lesson I took from this cartoon—and the reason why I had it hanging so visibly in my office—was that often there is a large difference between what we conceive and what we execute.

I've known many writers, including myself, who have great plans for great literary achievements, but find out in the execution that those great plans have shrunk. Sometimes we envision a book, but wind up with a 1200- to 2000-word magazine piece. A comedy writing friend of mine once said, "I started out to write a book and ended up with a pamphlet."

When that happens, you can't finish the book because a book doesn't really exist. Referring back to the previous item about starting your book with the proper preparation, the organization process you go through before beginning your book will help ensure that you have enough material for a complete book.

◆ ◆ ◆

Solution: Pay special attention to the recommendations in Chapter 5 (START CHIPPING AWAY) and give full consideration to jotting down all those ideas you might want to include in your book. If you stay focused on that brainstorming task, and don't quit gathering ideas too soon, you'll provide yourself with enough information to decide whether or not you have sufficient substance to fill a reasonably sized book.

4. You Start Your Book, but Keep Postponing It Until You Finally Abandon It

In the television writing business, writers would often go from staff to staff. Shows would be cancelled and new shows would be created. There were many good-byes in the profession. Of course, none of us would admit that they were "good-byes"; to us, they were more "Let's get together for lunch sometime." In effect, they were good-byes. We would part vowing to call and get together for lunch, but we'd put it off for a few weeks. Then we'd vow to call this week—*definitely*. But we wouldn't. Then we'd hit that point where it became embarrassing to call. The result was that those of us who vowed to "get together for lunch sometime," never got together for lunch.

That's what can happen with this book you're writing. You have fine intentions. You may go through the recommended planning and preparation. You may even get off to a good start by writing chapters one, two, and three. Then you decide to take a break. Heck, you're off to such a fine beginning that chapter four can wait a week. The following week you have a few problems at work or at home and chapter four is postponed again.

This can go on and on until chapters one, two, three, and the rest of your book are gathered up and put in a bottom drawer or some remote shelf and is abandoned. It's a sin of omission. You don't purposely stop writing your book; you simply keep pushing it back and back on your schedule and lower and lower on your list of priorities. In effect, you stop writing your book.

♦ ♦ ♦

Solution: The program I detail in this book will overcome this problem for you. It will require you to plan a definite writing schedule. More important, probably, it suggests that you create a *reasonable* writing schedule. That means that you are realistic in making your plans. Don't commit yourself to writing four chapters a week if you can only conveniently write one or two chapters a week. Be honest with yourself. Scheduling more than you can write is demoralizing. The demand will exhaust you. It may deflate you so much that abandoning your project is your only escape.

The process in this book advises that you work in a system of vacations and rewards. Perhaps you schedule one chapter a week for three weeks and then you give yourself some vacation time. Take the fourth week off. Don't work on the book, or work on a different aspect of the book—marketing, for example. This allows you to continue adhering to your schedule, but also it avoids that possible meltdown.

Also, you might crank in some rewards for your efforts. Suppose you're very enthused and write more than you've scheduled. What then? You have two choices. You can continue the momentum and write even more, which of course will put you ahead of schedule. That might pay dividends in the future. Or, you can allow yourself to relax. Do something that's fun. You've earned it; enjoy it.

The overriding principle here is that you should devise a writing schedule and then *adhere to it*. You want to keep the momentum of your writing going. A periodic vacation or a short span of rejuvenating relaxation won't destroy your momentum. Ignoring the writing schedule you've organized, could.

5. **Being Busy with Other Things—Like Your Day Job and Family and Home Projects—Can Make It Hard to Pick Up the Project and Know Where and How to Restart**

John Lennon once said "Life is what happens while we're busy making other plans." Reality can intrude on our fantasies quite easily. Sure, you want to write a book and you're dedicated to getting it completed, but things happen at work and things happen at home that take precedence. Even though you stay dedicated to your writing task, it's often difficult to get back into it and to regain the momentum you've built up.

No process can be so presumptuous as to pretend to override the demands of your work and your home life. Writing a book is nice, but providing for and raising a family is more important.

◆ ◆ ◆

Solution: The trick here is to capitalize on whatever free time you can afford for your writing. Maybe it's just a bit of time in the morning or staying up a tad later in the evening. If you can find any time, you can devote it to your writing schedule. Again, work it in reasonably. Overworking or exhausting yourself doesn't really help get your project completed. So, be realistic in planning your writing schedule around your demanding real-life priorities.

The problem with such a make-shift schedule is that it is more difficult to control the momentum. You not only have to goad yourself into writing, but you have to be able to pick it up and run with it as if you had never left it. The process outlined in this book can be helpful in that respect.

Films, you know, are not shot in sequence. They don't begin shooting the movie at the start and then go through it scene by scene until the ending credits. They plan the entire project because it's cheaper and quicker to shoot certain scenes in certain locations and with certain sets. Yet they must know how each of those scenes, even though shot out of sequence, will fit into the final flow of the film.

By planning and defining your book, outlining and describing the separate chapters, you create a comprehensive overall plan for your book. Regardless of which facet you're working on, you can envision how it fits in with the complete scheme.

This permits you to work on small portions of your project in any sequence and yet keep them blended with the general concept. It helps overcome the inertia of stopping and restarting.

6. Working in a Disorganized Fashion

Several years ago, I had the interior of my house painted. It was a traumatic experience. The work was disruptive, intrusive, and annoying. The job seemed to take forever. It didn't actually take forever, but it took longer than it should have taken because the work wasn't planned well. For instance, one day several workers painted the walls of the dining room. The next day, the man who was going to paint the louvered shutters on our windows opened them up and spray painted them. Now the freshly painted walls were striped with white paint. The dining room walls had to be repainted. Obviously, had the shutters been sprayed first, the walls would only have been painted once.

Any project that's not well planned and well executed will usually require corrections, revisions, and sometimes redoing work that's already been done. Aside from being inefficient, this can also be demoralizing.

If you have to rewrite chapters time and time again, you can easily get discouraged and perhaps abandon the entire project as being too troublesome. The ideal, of course, is to begin your writing, gather momentum, and allow that momentum to carry you through to completion. Good planning and scheduling can help with that.

◆ ◆ ◆

Solution: The procedures presented in this book guide you through the planning stages of your writing. They advise outlining your entire book and then devising a schedule that permits you to work in an organized fashion.

7. You Kill Your Enthusiasm for Your Project

You begin writing a book because you're enthused about what you have to say or the story you want to tell. That enthusiasm carries you through to the completion of your book. If that enthusiasm disappears, your dedication evaporates also and it becomes difficult to continue your writing.

But you can destroy your own enthusiasm. One way is by allowing too much time to pass between work sessions. We discussed this under item 4 above; you keep postponing the work until you eventually forsake it totally.

Another way to lose enthusiasm is to become discouraged with your efforts. As I said earlier, you begin this project loaded with enthusiasm and you envision a glorious result. But as you look at the work you're doing, you may begin to get discouraged. It's not quite as grand as you had hoped. You get demoralized, lose interest, and give up on the project.

◆ ◆ ◆

Solution: Review the solutions we discussed under item 4 earlier. By setting a reasonable, doable schedule *and by sticking to it*, you minimize the chances of losing your enthusiasm.

To avoid becoming discouraged with your efforts, be a little more forgiving of yourself. Chances are your first attempts may not live up to your grand anticipation. That's not unusual. However, you must avoid becoming too critical too early. Remember, this is a first draft. Resolve to get your thoughts on paper. They can be refined and rewritten later.

Also, be careful that you don't spend too much time at this stage criticizing and rewriting your text. That can be inhibiting. In the early days of my television writing career, the producers teamed me with a writer who was an obsessive rewriter. On our first day of working together, we began a comedy sketch. The process went something like this:

> We began by putting words in the character's mouth. "Hey, Pal, it's good to see you." Then my writing partner would rewrite that. "Good to see you, Pal. How are you doing?" Then he'd change his mind and suggest, "Long time, no see, good buddy. How are things?" Then he'd start rewriting and retyping that.
>
> I said, "Hold on. If you're going to rewrite each line of dialogue seven or eight times, we'll be here all day. Just type something in and let's move on to the next line."

So, don't spend too much time worrying about each line, each paragraph, or even each chapter at this point of the process. Continue writing in order to keep the momentum alive. There will come a time for evaluating, revising, and fine-tuning later.

Also, this program recommends some pre-planning for each chapter before you begin writing it. You'll see that in Chapter 8 (WRITE A CHAPTER) and Chapter 12 (WRITING YOUR BOOK CHAPTER BY CHAPTER). Thinking through a chapter before writing it helps make your writing more coherent, more free-flowing, and more consistent with the ideas you want to convey. This will produce better writing and less discouragement.

8. Allowing Others to Kill Your Enthusiasm

Writers can be insecure. Once I worked on writing a sitcom pilot show. At an early rehearsal, the head of the network came in to review the show. He and his assistant had plentiful notes for rewriting. The network head would say something like, "I want these kids to be troublesome, but at the same time somewhat agreeable." His lackey would then rephrase this by saying, "You want them to be rebelliously cooperative." And all of us writers would note that. Then the boss would comment, "I'd like the characters to be shy, yet persuasive." The assistant would repeat that thought saying, "You want them to be aggressively withdrawn." We'd note it.

At the end of the day, we writers wound up with a script full of oxymoronic notes that were impossible to understand, let alone rewrite. Nevertheless, we worked on revising the script until the early morning hours. At about two in the morning, we had only one more joke to re-write into the script. Finally, someone ad-libbed something and we all laughed. We said, "Type that quickly and let's get out of here."

However, before typing the line, the writer, as a joke, asked the over-night cleaning lady who was mopping the office floor what she thought of the line. Without missing a beat or a swipe of her mop she said, "I think you're reaching a bit."

We immediately dropped that line and began searching for another.

That's how insecure writers can be.

The same could happen to you with your manuscript. Show it to friends and one negative comment could destroy your enthusiasm and convince you to drop the project. A rejection from a publisher or an agent can quickly discourage us. (We'll talk a bit about rejection later in this text. It is an unavoidable part of the writing life, but it's not always as negative as we assume.) If this is a possibility, though, you might want to finish your project before even exposing it to the marketplace. Sure, it would be nice to sell a project before it's written, but is it worth risk-ing the abandonment of the whole manuscript because someone doesn't want to buy it at that time? That's a decision each writer has to make.

◆ ◆ ◆

Solution: Be protective of your work. Remember that your book is a work in progress. Keep it away from others until it's complete. If you show the work to Aunt Mabel and she says, "Well, it didn't knock my socks off," it might be the end of that book you've always wanted to write.

Aunt Mabel probably doesn't know as much about writing as you do, so why listen to her? In fact, why allow her to comment at all?

If you need help with your project, go to good writers or thinkers that you trust. Allow them to offer suggestions. To all others, your work is off-limits.

These are some of the problems that may keep you from finishing your book. There may be others that are specifically yours. We writers can be very creative in finding reasons why we can't finish a project.

Try to find the answers to the big "Why"—why you're not completing the book that you're so enthused about. Analyze them and find a cure. The most important item on your writing agenda right now is to get your book *finished*. That's what my writing program is all about. Are you ready to roll up your sleeves and get to it?

CHAPTER 2

NO ONE CAN WRITE A BOOK

THAT'S RIGHT—NO ONE CAN WRITE A BOOK. Charles Dickens couldn't. Stephen King can't. J.K. Rowling can't either. You're probably saying to yourself, "Wait a minute. I know Charles Dickens has written a book. I had to read *A Tale of Two Cities* in school. I not only had to read it, I had to give an oral book report on it. I distinctly remember starting my speech by saying, '*A Tale of Two Cities* by Charles Dickens.' How could I say that if Dickens never wrote a book?"

All right, you've got a point there. Having won that concession, you might continue with, "And J.K. Rowling is now one of the wealthiest women in the world. They wouldn't be paying her that kind of money if she never wrote a book. She must have written a book."

OK, again, you make a good argument. Recognizing that you're on a roll, you say: "Stephen King has not only written several best sellers, but they've made movies out of them. How can they make a movie out of something that you claim he never wrote?" Again, a valid argument.

Nevertheless, I still maintain that no one can write a book. Charles Dickens couldn't. Stephen King can't. J.K. Rowling, despite her glorious advances and royalty checks, can't either. (By now you're probably shaking your head in disbelief, and you maybe feeling a touch of pity for this befuddled author.)

Let's get away from writing books for a moment and allow me to offer the following hypothetical to help illustrate my logic:

Suppose you go to an elegant, slightly over-priced steak house for dinner. You glance over the menu and decide on a 16-ounce Porterhouse steak. You order it medium rare, and the waiter graciously takes your order and relays it to the kitchen. Later he returns with a glorious looking slice of meat, still sizzling from the grill and cooked exactly the way you like it. I now maintain that you can't eat that 16-ounce Porterhouse.

You say, "What are you? Nuts? I'm starving and this steak looks promiscuously delicious. I paid $40 plus tax and tip for this hunk of beef and I'm going to eat it right down to the final 16th scrumptious ounce."

I still say that you can't eat a 16-ounce Porterhouse steak. Am I wrong? Well, no and yes.

When the waiter brought your plate, did you notice the steak knife he set down next to it? Why did he do this? Because he knows, as I do, that you can't eat a 16-ounce Porterhouse steak. All you can do is use that specially sharpened knife to carve that steak into reasonably sized chunks. You then proceed to eat one delicious morsel after another until you've devoured with great relish that the delicious, $40 chunk of meat.

In the same way, Dickens, Rowling, and King, cannot write a complete book. They can only write a part of a book. Eventually, I admit, they do put all the pieces together to form a finished manuscript. That's why you could present an oral book report on *A Tale of Two Cities*. It's why you can enjoy a movie based on a Stephen King novel. It's why J.K. Rowling can with good conscience cash her generous advance and royalty checks.

Now, I realize that you're shaking your head with even more pity and asking why we went through this exercise in semantics and logic. The reason is because this idea forms the basis for my program for starting and completing the book you want to write.

The task of authoring a complete book is daunting. In fact, it's formidable enough to scare many would-be authors away. Completing a book is a huge task and takes so much time, we tell ourselves, that it's hardly worth beginning. We continue to keep it as a long range goal in our minds, rather than converting it to a task that we can start right now.

On the other hand, though, if we persuade ourselves to write only a small part of the book, we can start that tiny task and finish it *now*. At least then we've written part of a book, which as I stated earlier, is all that Charles Dickens, Stephen King, and J. K. Rowling could do.

So the first step in starting and completing the book you want to write is to recognize and admit that you can't write an entire book. You must agree that you can write only a portion of the book at a time. Once you understand that, you can begin planning your writing project so that each piece of the book you complete will fit into your overall plan.

Obviously, it would be silly to just write chunks of a book that have no relation to one another. You'd wind up with a hodge-podge of a manuscript. Just as a builder begins with detailed blueprints of the home he is constructing before he even pours the foundation, you must design your book to detailed specifications before you attack the writing. With blueprints, the contractor can now work on various facets of the home, knowing that eventually it will all come together. You the writer, armed with a detailed plan based on the step-by-step instructions in this book, can work on various facets of your book, knowing that it will become a coherent manuscript.

There are four important attributes that you, the writer, must bring to this process of starting and completing your book. We'll discuss the importance of these components, and how they affect each step in the writing process, as we progress through the program. For now, though, let's briefly discuss each one in particular.

- **Focus:** This is the ability to concentrate on a small part of your overall task. The smaller the segment is and the more you can focus on just that one area, the better your results will be. Focus is using the steak knife to carve your Porterhouse into reasonably sized morsels so that you can effectively chew and savor each bite of your $40 prize. Trying to stuff the entire chunk of beef into your mouth would not only be exceedingly difficult, it would be decidedly unappetizing were it even possible. The tiny pieces are much more manageable and definitely more tasty.

  So, rather than attack the overall project of writing a book, you focus on smaller, bite-sized chunks, tackling them one at a time. By doing this you make your efforts more productive and the results more effective—and more flavorful.

- **Organization:** In order to break your work into bite-sized chunks, you must first plan your attack. Just as the aforementioned contractor needs blueprints before beginning to build a house, you as a writer must lay out a blueprint for your finished book. You must formulate a plan that will guarantee that when the various parts of your writing are finally assembled, they will form a logical, interesting, complete whole. The "whole," of course, being the sum of its "parts"—the book.

- **Momentum:** This is the force that carries you along in your task until it is completed. It should be relatively continuous. Oh, you'll have good days and not-so-good days, but you should try to maintain a productive pace. Stopping and starting your writing is not always conducive to completing a book because sometimes when you stop, you don't start again.

Also, momentum helps to keep your writing style uniform. If your writing is continuous, your writing style will be consistent. However, if you write chapters 1 and 2 now and then write chapters 3 and 4 half a year later, your writing style may change dramatically. In fact, the total concept of your book could change.

It's best to start your project and keep the activity and the momentum going until you finish it.

■ **Discipline:** Writing is not easy. William Styron expressed it well: "Let's face it, writing is hell." It demands discipline. We can't work only when the spirit and the flesh are willing. We should work when the muse visits us, of course, but we must work even when the muse seems to have abandoned us and is shuffling down the street towards the local pub.

My program requires you to provide a stiff dose of discipline, as your first task is to fully execute the entire planning process before you begin writing, despite the fact that you're probably eager to get to the keyboard to start pounding out paragraphs. Discipline restrains your enthusiasm until you're absolutely prepared to release it effectively.

You'll depend on discipline in order to create a workable schedule, one that is —demanding but realistic. That same discipline will also guide you in adhering to your schedule, regardless of exhaustion, boredom, and other demands on your time.

Discipline will give you the strength to continue on to completion. After all, *completing* your book is the entire purpose of this writing adventure you're determined to begin.

Writing a book is not an easy task, yet with planning and discipline, you'll build a momentum that will propel you toward the finish line and that can make the entire process enjoyable and rewarding. The struggles you'll endure along the way will all seem worth it once you hold that completed manuscript, and later perhaps that bound book with your name on it, in your hands. Charles Dickens felt that thrill. J.K. Rowling and Stephen King know how exciting that feels. You will, too.

THREE IMPORTANT ATTITUDES

WE'RE ALMOST READY TO GO INTO THE DETAILS of the program that will get you working on your manuscript and, in time, writing and completing your book. Before we dive into the program, though, let's quickly discuss three general attitudes that are important in helping you follow the process this book presents. I discussed these earlier in connection with reasons why books don't get written. However, they're so important to my system that it seems beneficial to expand on them now before we actually begin the system together.

1. Get It on Paper

The first attitude—almost an admonition—is to *get it on paper*. It may seem redundant to say that, in order to write a book, you have to write. Nevertheless, some people keep postponing the actual writing. They seem to delay it forever, then wonder why the book doesn't get written. Your book will not be written until you *write* it.

> Several years ago I hosted an annual comedy writers seminar. The various sessions included lectures, lessons, writing exercises, writing games, and question-and-answer periods with many established television writers. At one lecture, the speaker presented a challenge to the attendees. He suggested several exercises that they might do once they got home from the seminar that would sharpen their comedy-writing skills.

> The following year, one of the attendees returned to the seminar. He spoke to this particular faculty member and said, "That series of exercises you handed out last year was fantastic. I've attended many writing conferences and that advice you gave us and the work you assigned was the most beneficial I've ever heard." The speaker said, "Good. I'm glad you feel that way. How did you make out with it?" The aspiring writer said, "Oh, I never got around to actually doing it."
>
> That's typical of so many of us. We know we have a book in us. We desperately want to write it. The only drawback is that we keep putting off the actual writing.

My program recommends that you plan your writing, but it also suggests that you do some actual writing. You must get something on paper.

A colleague of mine on the Bob Hope writing staff expressed this idea well. He said, "You can turn in *good* jokes to Bob Hope. And you can turn in *bad* jokes to Bob Hope. But you can't turn in *no* jokes to Bob Hope."

What he was saying was that whether a writer was creatively inspired or not, that writer still had to write something. If the writer was "on" that day, the jokes would be brilliant. If the writer was "off" that day, the jokes would be ordinary. But in either case, the writer would have to put *something* on paper to physically hand to Bob Hope.

The same is true for this book you want to write. Some days, you'll be magnificent; on other days you'll be not so magnificent. But to complete your book, it's imperative that you get words on paper. Those words and thoughts don't have to be perfect just yet. My program, you'll learn, allows ample time for rewriting and fine-tuning. *But you can't correct, revise, or polish something that doesn't exist.* You need words on paper before you can rewrite them.

2. Avoid Being Too Critical of Your Writing

Here's the second attitude you should adopt: Resist being too critical of your writing. A big factor in this process of starting and completing a book is gaining momentum and keeping it going. That's what will carry you through your project from the blank pages to the final manuscript. Obsessing with getting everything perfect in the first draft can sometimes destroy that momentum. Rather than write, you concern yourself more with how good your writing could be if you could only get around to actually writing it. Certainly, as you put your thoughts on paper, you try to be as eloquent and precise as you can. Write as wonderfully and as effectively as you know how. However, if you're somewhat dissatisfied with your choice of vocabulary or your similes and metaphors, don't allow that to distract you from your primary purpose—to get your book written.

So bring all of your energy, talent, and focus to each segment of your book that you write, but avoid being overly judgmental. Do not sacrifice your momentum!

3. Worry About the Fine Points Later

The third attitude is that you should not be preoccupied at this point of the writing with punctuation, grammar, vocabulary, or writing technique. This, again, promotes momentum. As a comedy writer, I created many current events gags. There was a time when I prided myself on being one of the few people who could correctly spell the name "Khrushchev." I knew that it had three "h's" in it, and I knew where they went. Yet, if I handed in good jokes that had the Russian leader's name spelled with only two "h's," the gag would still get laughs. My spelling had little to do with the comedic value of the joke line.

So long as you get your ideas across (and get your book actually written), all the flaws can be corrected later. If you omit a comma, you can add it later. If you have used a comma and you decide later that a semi-colon would be better, you can change it. If you feel that a certain word is more descriptive than the one you originally put into the text, use the more effective word. As I mentioned, my program encourages reviewing and revising your work. You'll spot many of these wording and punctuation errors as you read through you manuscript. Also, if you have a publishing company, they'll assign a trained editor to look for any mistakes and suggest improvements. However, trying to incorporate all of this perfection into your first draft can be cumbersome, and it just might turn out to be a momentum killer.

So, to quickly review, at this stage of your writing, determine:
- To get it on paper
- To avoid being too critical of your writing
- Not to obsess over punctuation, grammar, vocabulary, or writing technique…yet.

None of these suggestions are meant to encourage lazy, sloppy, or "easy" writing. They're simply designed to keep you at the keyboard, turning out paragraphs and pages.

This program for starting and completing your book demands preparation. I recommend not only that you plan your entire book, but that you organize your thoughts before writing the individual chapters. With solid, extensive preparation, you should be able to bring much skill and finesse to your writing, even at this first-draft stage. All I'm proposing now is that you be wary of focusing too much attention to the finer points. You don't want that to negatively affect your output. It's more important that you stick to your prepared writing schedule and maintain that all-important momentum.

DEFINE YOUR BOOK

With the suggestions from Chapter 3 in mind, you're ready to begin writing your book. However, the writing you produce for the initial task I have for you will most likely not be included in your manuscript—yet even so, you will find that it will influence every word in your book.

What you should do now is define the book that you intend to write. Here are the elements that you should include in your book's definition:

- A description of the book
- Your reasons why you feel this book should be written
- Why you know you're the person who should write this book
- Who you're writing this book for
- Why your book is different from those already available on the subject (if any).

Let's now discuss each of these elements more completely.

WRITE A DESCRIPTION OF THE BOOK

At this point, your book is a concept that exists in your mind. It may be quite vivid to you, but it still is only a concept. The image you hold in your mind now may not be the same as the one you will see days, weeks, or months from now. The concept can gradually change. However, when you translate your idea to the written page, it becomes locked in. What you put on paper today will not change after several days, weeks, or months. It will always remain as written.

This doesn't mean that the book is forever unchangeable, of course. If you come up with a new idea or a variation on the concept later that you feel improves your book, you can always incorporate it into your project. Your book remains flexible until you print it and put it on the bookstore shelves. But writing your idea down now does guarantee that you will be in charge of any changes, and you will decide when improvements are needed. If you allow the book to remain a vague concept in your mind, that concept can change without you even being aware of it. That can be confusing and disruptive to the completion of your book.

Remember, I've said that completing a book is a big task. It's difficult to get the entire package contained in your mind. By defining your book idea now and getting it on paper, you create a solid reference point. You have a blueprint that you can always return to for guidance.

So, your first step in the process that will result in the completion of your book is quite straightforward: Describe it. Tell yourself what the book is about. You needn't worry much about style or technique with this exercise. This is merely a record of the basic concept of the book you're about to write, and it will be something you'll refer to often. Its primary purpose is to keep you focused on the original concept of your book. **Again, in a concise manner, simply tell yourself what your book is about.**

As examples, here are brief descriptions of a few of the books I've written. This first one is the description I wrote for my book on comedy writing:

Comedy Writing Step by Step: *This book will encourage and inspire those people who might want to consider writing comedy to give it a try. It will reassure aspiring comedy writers that the profession is open to them and that certain aspects of comedy writing can be taught. It is based on the idea that the joke is the basic building block of comedy. By mastering the joke-writing technique, writers can use that to compile stand-up material, and later grow into writing sketches, sitcom scripts, film scripts, plays, humorous articles, and humorous fiction or nonfiction books.*

This book will offer lessons on researching and analyzing topics to write about. It will suggest methods to get the joke ideas flowing. Also, it will suggest ways to organize the writing into logical comedy routines. In short, it will guide the reader through the comedy writing process from the blank page to the finished monologue.

The book will also offer suggestions for marketing one's material and for building a career as a comedy writer.

This next example is from my book on "Creativity":

Unleashing Your Creativity After 50: *John Lennon once said that life is what happens while we're busy making other plans. This book will encourage people who have reached the half-century mark to pursue some creative activities. These might be avocations that they dreamed of as youngsters, before life and reality intervened. Or, they may be new adventures that they have never tried before. The book will suggest that now—after 50—is the ideal time to experiment with them.*

This book will offer many reasons why now is the perfect time. It will list the advantages of pursuing creative adventures. It will also rebut some of the traditional excuses for not remaining creative. It will offer advice on how to begin to search for new, creative activities.

Also, one chapter will offer 101 creative activities that the reader might pursue.

Both of the above ideas were how-to books. However, the same can be done for fiction. Here's a brief description of an allegorical novel that I wrote:

Breakfasts with Archangel Shecky: *In this novel, a part-time stand-up comedian from Philadelphia is not having much success with his career. He's about ready to abandon the goal when he meets up with a gentleman who claims that he can help him advance. The gentleman also claims to be his Guardian Angel.*

The two form an unlikely friendship, with insults flying back and forth. The supposed angel is one who likes to drink scotch, eat all of the Philadelphia fast food he can get hold of, and who dislikes, and avoids, picking up either bar tabs or restaurant checks.

During several late-night snack sessions and early-morning break-fasts, the angel gives the struggling performer solid advice on developing his comedy and achieving success in the profession.

The performer is naturally skeptical about his mentor's angelic claims and, in fact, demands proof. The mentor can't or won't deliver that. Yet, the comic is somehow drawn to not only listen to the "angel's" advice, but also to experiment with the lessons and assignments he offers.

Is the mentor really a Guardian Angel? Do his suggestions work? These questions are all answered by the novel's end.

Getting a description of your book on paper is important because it helps to lock down the concept that you want to write. As I mentioned earlier, any concept that is not recorded, that is purely mental, can begin to shift and change. You might find yourself, after many weeks of work, writing a different book than the one you thought you began. Maybe the new concept is better. That's certainly possible. Nevertheless, it should be a new concept that you are aware of. The changes should be ones that you are in control of.

Also, having a firm definition helps keep you focused on your project. It's often easy to slip into tangential areas. Rather than writing the book you want to write, you may find that you're writing *around* it. Text that goes flying off in several directions can be confusing to the reader and can weaken the impact of the idea that you really want to convey.

To see more examples of book descriptions, you could check Amazon. com. Most of the books listed on that website have a paragraph or two telling what the book is about. These can be worthwhile guides in writing your own description.

LIST YOUR REASONS WHY YOU FEEL THIS BOOK SHOULD BE WRITTEN

Enthusiasm is a big factor in completing any project. You're certainly enthused about your book right now. You're enthused because this is a book you genuinely want to write. Capture that enthusiasm by telling yourself, on paper, why you're so excited about your project.

Writing a book is a formidable and time-consuming task. It has some gloriously satisfying moments and some depressing ones. Be prepared: There will be moments when you question why you're putting yourself through such torment. As has most every person who's written a book, you'll ask yourself, "Why am I doing this?" The reason why you're doing it can be found in your book's definition. It's written right there for you to review and recapture, and to inspire you anew.

As an example, let's refer back to my book, *Comedy Writing Step by Step:*

This book is being written for those who have a desire to write comedy—either as a hobby, a part-time income, or as a professional career—but have no idea where to find information or how to begin. This book will offer them some direction so that they can at least try the craft to see if they can turn out usable comedy material.

That was my reason for writing that book. Why are you writing yours?

DESCRIBE WHY YOU'RE THE PERSON TO WRITE THIS BOOK

List the unique qualifications that you bring to this project. Note the distinctive point of view that you have on the topic you're writing about. Mention your credibility in the field and your credentials. Be honest in describing why you're a person who should be listened to.

This doesn't mean that you must be an expert in your field or a recognized authority. It might simply mean that you have an interest in whatever subject you're writing about. That interest might inspire you to do some research in the field and analyze that research. The observations and conclusions you come to, you believe, are beneficial to your potential readers.

As I mentioned above, completing your book may be a struggle from time to time. Just as you must rejuvenate your enthusiasm periodically, you should also remind yourself that you bring something special to this book, and that you are the only person who can write it the way you envision it. Turning back to this written definition will accomplish that for you.

DEFINE WHO YOU'RE WRITING THIS BOOK FOR

Your audience influences your execution of this project. Again, completing a book is a large task. It's easy to become sidetracked and start handing out information that is either too confusing to your audience, too basic for your audience, or irrelevant to your potential readership. And, of course, what is basic to one reader might be too complex for another. If you define your readership well, you'll be able to gear your text to that audience.

A student in one of my writing classes was a travel guide for many years. Naturally, he had countless humorous, and sometimes near-disastrous, tales to tell. He wanted to write this book because friends and relatives enjoyed the stories so much that they felt they would make a funny, interesting, entertaining volume. It would. However, the author also felt that the book could be a practical instruction manual for other travel guides. In effect, it would be a how-to manual for people in the travel profession. It could be. The author also felt that the material would be useful to vacationers. It could suggest ways to plan for a vacation. It would be useful in getting the most practical prices, planning what to pack, and so on. It could definitely accomplish that goal, also.

However, you can readily see the complications all of these goals wrapped in one volume would present. Does the author write to entertain the reader? Should the tales told be used to educate other travel guides? Are the pages designed to inform travelers of helpful hints in planning their trips?

Knowing which of these three groups of readers the author wanted to communicate with would help in planning the book, deciding which material to include and exclude, and eventually, in the writing of the text. For example, in the definition of my book, *Comedy Writing Step by Step*, I explicitly noted that it would be written for *aspiring* comedy writers, beginning humorists, and writers who had a desire to write comedy but no idea where to begin. In writing this volume, I was tempted to include chapters on writing pilot shows for TV. However, realizing that this book was written for beginners, it was obvious that this advice was unnecessary...or maybe premature. Networks rarely purchase pilot shows from beginners, so this sort of advice would be beyond the scope of my targeted readers.

> As an aside to further illustrate the importance of knowing your audience, Bob Hope once called his writers and asked for some gags that he could present in a show he was doing for a group of psychologists. Psychology jokes are kind of a dream for joke writers. Forgive the pun, but we could go as crazy as we wanted. All of the staff turned in plenty of material.
>
> As the head-writer, I got a follow up call from Mr. Hope after he had received the gags. He said, "Gene, I was mistaken. It's not a psychologists' convention; it's a chiropractors' convention."
>
> How many of those original gags do you suppose were usable?
>
> So it's important to know who you are writing for.

WHY IS YOUR BOOK DIFFERENT FROM THOSE ALREADY AVAILABLE ON THE SUBJECT (IF ANY)?

If you do some research on the topic or area you want to write about, you'll discover that there most likely are similar books already in the bookstores. You now want to add another one. If yours doesn't offer anything new or different, though, it's unnecessary. Another volume that simply restates what these other books contain serves no real purpose.

It's wise at this point of the process to remind yourself of the uniqueness of your volume; this will help you remember what aspects to emphasize as you write.

Keep in mind, though, that in this definition, you're claiming only that your book is *different*. It's not necessarily *better*. If you include this distinction in your query letter or book proposal (and we'll talk more about those later), you want to avoid criticizing or putting down other books. Simply state the ways in which your book either adds information to the subject you're dealing with or treats the subject differently.

As an example, I wrote a book called *Successful Stand-up Comedy*. There were books already available that were written by former or current stand-up comedians. They had experience developing their acts, finding employment in comedy clubs, and appearing before live audiences. I didn't have that background. Nevertheless, I did have experience in comedy that was unique. I had been hired by several performers to stand backstage, in the wings, or even in the audience to monitor the material and delivery of these comics. In that sense, my book couldn't claim to be *better* than those written by stand-up comics. It was, though, a much different approach…and a beneficial one.

> There is a man named Doyle Brunson who is not only a renowned poker player but who has also written what most experts consider the ultimate book on Poker Strategy—*Doyle Brunson's Super System (A Course in Power Poker)*. You could read Brunson's book and learn all the strategy you would need to become a poker whiz. You might also write a book of your own on poker strategy. However, if Brunson has said all that can be said about expert poker playing, what can you add to that?
>
> Consider this, though—Doyle Brunson plays with the poker experts. His game plan factors that in. His advice is for when you're playing against the great poker talents in the world.
>
> Your book might be different in that you analyze his playing strategies and utilize them so that you can beat the "toads" that you play against in your friendly Friday night poker get together. Many of the schemes you suggest in your book would get shot down if you played the experts, yet they may make you a few bucks playing against less accomplished players. You may adapt Brunson's techniques to your specific situation.
>
> You should see then that your book is not better than Doyle Brunson's. It is different, though.

There are two ways that you can handle the writing of this book definition—you can write it purely as a reminder to yourself or you can write it as something that may be included as part of your marketing approach. If you're writing it purely as a reminder to yourself, then you needn't worry too much about style or technique. Any writing that gets the ideas across to you is acceptable. It's like an informal memo to yourself, the author.

In Chapter 11 (GET YOUR BOOK TO THE MARKETPLACE), I'll discuss how you might get your book circulating to agents or publishers while you're still writing it. With that idea in mind, you may want to write this definition so that it can included in your marketing plans. If you decide to do that, you should rewrite this definition more formally. Compose it using proper style, accurate vocabulary, perfect spelling, and acceptable punctuation. Write it as carefully as you would write the text. (You also may want to glance ahead to Chapter 11 to learn some techniques for writing an appropriate query letter or book proposal.)

At this point, though, the choice is yours—write it for your own purposes or write it for submission to the marketplace.

CHAPTER 5

START CHIPPING AWAY

THERE'S A STORY TOLD THAT SUPPOSEDLY EXPLAINS how Michelangelo carved his magnificent *David*. The theory is that Michelangelo started with a block of marble and then chipped away everything that didn't look like David. The tale is mythical, of course, but it is apropos here because that's how you'll begin this book-writing adventure—by chipping away at the project until it begins to look like a book.

In this step of the program, you'll begin *shaping* your book. Remember, I said that no one can write a book. One can only write a part of a book, which is how you'll begin to shape your book—by writing only part of it. And it will be a very small part indeed. Just as we mentioned earlier that you carve a 16-ounce porterhouse steak into bite-sized chunks, now you'll begin writing your book by creating small, manageable chunks.

SKETCH OUT AN INITIAL IDEA

Start with *one* chunk.

Let's assume for the moment that you want to write a book about sculpting portraits in clay. Where do you start chipping away at that? Well, think of something—*anything*—that you want to tell your readers. Jot that something down and, while you're thinking about it, jot down a few supporting ideas. There—you've now begun to shape your book.

Let's say that the first thought that pops into your mind is that the readers should know what tools they'll need to work in clay. Fine. You jot down that idea and label it "Tools You'll Need." You begin to fill out the idea by noting several of the basic tools that are essential. You may also make a note to tell the readers where they can obtain these implements and approximately how much they'll cost. Maybe you'll make a note to explain briefly how these tools are used and for what purpose. You might even remind yourself of an entertaining anecdote about someone who tried to get by with the wrong tools.

There. You have now noted one major idea—quite possibly the basis for a full chapter—of your book. It may not be the first chapter, but at this point that's not important. It is the stuff of a chapter and you have got it recorded.

SKETCH OUT ANOTHER IDEA

Now, think of something else you want to tell the reader about sculpting in clay.

Let's imagine that you realize that the eyes are a particular challenge in carving a clay portrait. OK, you label your next segment "Shaping the Eyes." You note any ideas that would support this chapter, e.g., eye-sculpting techniques used by the masters of the craft, major mistakes to avoid when shaping eyes, etc. This probably wouldn't be Chapter 2 in your manuscript, but it will probably find a home in your book somewhere.

ONE BY ONE, SKETCH OUT THE OTHER IDEAS YOU HAVE FOR YOUR BOOK

You now have ideas in place for two chapters. They're certainly not finished products; they're merely notes to yourself at this point. But they are parts of the book you intend to write.

Now, continue to think of things you want to say. Jot them down and add any supporting ideas that pop into your head. Remember again that you're not writing the entire book; you're writing *parts* of your book. The idea here is to let ideas flow from your mind onto the paper. Get as many concepts as you want to cover jotted down so that you can organize and arrange them later in this process of completing your manuscript.

Continue to focus and work on this project, one concept at a time, until you've noted virtually everything you want to say to the readers in your book. Keep at it; make this list as complete as possible. This is not a one- or two-hour project. It may take days, even weeks, of focusing and making notes before you're convinced that you have included all that you want to include. So focus on this one phase of the process now, until your thoughts are recorded.

Eventually, you'll have on paper all of the concepts that you want to convey in your book. At this point, you're not concerned with which chapters will go where. Even so, through this exercise you will start to see the skeleton of your entire volume. You can now manipulate chapters, arrange them into a logical sequence, and perhaps divide the book into meaningful sections. All of this, though, happens after you get your thoughts translated from your mind to the page.

Let me give you an idea of the process by illustrating with one part of my book, *Comedy Writing Step by Step.* One of the ideas I wanted to convey to the readers was to debunk the myth that comedy could not be taught or learned. "If you weren't born with the skill," many said, "you could not acquire it." This was nonsense to me. Therefore, the first thing I wanted to say to my readers was that they could learn to write comedy. The heading for the first concept I jotted down was "Comedy Writing Can Be Learned." The notes I made to support that idea looked like this:

1. Tell the story of the contradiction in a certain book I read
2. Mention art schools, running coaches, basketball's big men camps
3. Experience is a great teacher
4. Tricks of the trade
5. You can teach yourself

I realize that these notes are cryptic and have clear meaning only to the person who wrote them. Therefore, let me explain my shorthand notes in more detail so that you can understand this process I'm talking about more clearly.

Note number 1 ("Tell the story of the contradiction in a certain book I read") is a reminder to myself to begin the writing of this particular idea with something I read in a book on comedy writing. On the first page, the author said that no one could teach anyone how to write comedy. He maintained it was a natural-born talent that no one could learn. Then two pages later, he paid tribute to "The man who taught me everything I know about comedy writing." If no one could teach comedy writing, I wondered, how did his mentor accomplish it?

Note number 2 is to remind me of my response to people who ask, "Can you learn to write funny?" The implication again is that it's a talent that can't be acquired if you don't already have it. I mention that some people are born with artistic skills and some aren't. Yet there are art schools and degree courses in college that teach "Art." You can't *teach* speed. A person is either fast or not fast. Yet every baseball team has a coach that tutors the players on running the bases. Certainly, you can't acquire height. You're as tall as you are. Yet, in basketball they have "Big Men Camps" that teach the taller players how to use their height—in effect, how to play even taller. So, certain skills are gifts, yet anyone can learn to improve even the most fundamental talent.

Note number 3 tells about writers who boast of their experience. The idea is that since they have been at the profession longer than others, they know more about it. They are more skilled. They have *learned* over the years. That is true. However, if a person learns over the years, that implies that those years have *taught* that person something. That person can then recount those experiences and others can learn from them.

Note number 4 reminds me that there are certain shortcuts that can be learned. Even if they have nothing to do with the actual talent of a person, they can help that person write more quickly, or effectively, or more productively. This, in essence, is learning.

Note number 5 is a note to myself to assure the readers that they can teach themselves. They can listen to comedians, read humorous articles, watch funny movies and plays. The greatest instructor to someone who wants to learn to write television comedy is the TV set that sits in the corner of the living room.

That's what the succinct notes on my sheet of paper meant to me when I jotted them down. I caution you that at this stage you needn't go into such detail as I just did. (I listed the expansion of my notes here just to illustrate the point.) In fact, it's probably counterproductive to dwell too much on the details. Right now, you want to collect and record the important thoughts that you want to include in your manuscript. That's the task at hand. Concentrating on the details or explanations—except for short, succinct reminders—can distract you from that chore.

It can also slow you down and inhibit the planning of the entire project. For instance, if you were planning to build your dream house, you'd have to develop plans. Suppose you're planning the kitchen of this new home and you get carried away. You go into minute details of that kitchen. Finally, you might decide that since you're on a roll, you might as well get some lumber, a few nails, and start building that part of the house.

That would be a mistake because not only does the planning of the kitchen have to be consistent with the plans for the rest of the house, but the building of that kitchen is probably dependent on some of the construction for the rest of the house being in place.

The warning here is to restrain yourself. Focus on those things you want to say in your book. Get those thoughts on paper. Support them with any ideas you have that might help you later in your project. But don't try to write the entire book, or even try to write part of the book at this stage. Plan your project completely before you tackle the text. You'll find it'll much more efficient that way.

Besides, you don't have to go into fine details now. In my writing program, you'll return to these thoughts at least three more times before you begin the formal writing of them. Here are the three steps you'll go through as you proceed through this program:

First, you'll decide whether each thought should be a complete chapter of the book, or if it might be combined with other thoughts in order to create a complete chapter. You might decide that some of these ideas should be dropped entirely as being inconsistent with the full project. (I'll discuss this in the next chapter of this book.)

Second, when these thoughts do become chapters, either in full or in part, you'll write a brief description of each chapter so that you can use it as a guide in your final writing. I deal with this in Chapter 7 (DESCRIBE EACH OF YOUR CHAPTERS).

Third, as part of your preparation for writing each chapter, my program suggests that you allow a fair amount of time to review your notes and your brief chapter descriptions, and that you make *full* notes as an outline for the actual writing of the text. I discuss this fully in Chapter 8 (WRITE A CHAPTER) and Chapter 12 (WRITING YOUR BOOK CHAPTER BY CHAPTER).

So with that little peek ahead, you see that there will be plenty of time to fill in the details. By proceeding in an orderly and restrained fashion, you will avoid duplicating tasks and the necessity to go back and rewrite or make extensive changes. At this phase of the program, all you want is a comprehensive list of your thoughts and ideas that might become chapters in your final manuscript. You'll eventually analyze and organize this list into a usable outline for your book.

> Here's an exercise that students in my classes have found helpful. It allows you to test this procedure and also to check how thorough you were in handling it. Each state has laws governing driving. Imagine that you were asked to write the driver's manual for your particular state.
>
> Briefly go through what items you would include. You'd have to consider traffic lights, solid or flashing. You'd have to think about the different lines painted on the road and what they allow and disallow. How about different colors painted on curbs? What do they mean and what do they prohibit?
>
> You should take time to briefly consider other areas that you might write about in order to explain fully the traffic laws of your state.

> Each state also issues a driving manual. You could now obtain a copy and check to see how thoroughly you dealt with this assignment.
>
> It's good practice and it might help you to realize how diligently you must focus on this phase of your planning in order to produce a full and complete outline for your own book.

METHODS FOR RECORDING YOUR IDEAS

How should you record your notes as you work your way through the exercise in this chapter? Should you write them on paper? Should you record them digitally? That's pretty much a personal preference. Some writers prefer long-hand notes; others prefer using a computer. Let me give you my preferences and you can use them or substitute your own versions.

I usually write out the original notes in longhand on lined paper. Using this method, I do a better job of capturing thoughts than when I'm at a keyboard. It allows me more time to "meditate" and to think about the ideas.

Also, I can write all over the paper, adding new elements and getting them placed properly by circling them and then drawing a quick arrow to where I want them. I just seem to have more of a hands-on feel for the concepts when I do it this way. Again, though, this is not a particular requirement of this program. Get your thoughts down any way that is effective for you.

Continuing on with my personal approach, once I have an idea captured, I'll convert it to a 3 x 5 index card. I'll put the main heading of the idea at the very bottom and then make my notes on the front and back of the card. Later on, when we talk about organizing your list, this index card idea can be very helpful. It allows me to see all of the ideas laid out before me, either on a table or pinned to a bulletin board. Also, I can move each of the individual cards to a new location in the overall sequence.

Again, though, many people are sufficiently proficient on the computer that rearranging the segments in a computer program is a snap. It's each writer's choice. Just keep in mind that since we will be rearranging these concepts, combining some, eliminating others, and in general reshaping the overall format of the book, it's important that these ideas we've gathered so far can be easily moved around.

SAMPLE IDEA CARDS

Let me give you a few examples of these idea cards that I have generated in connection with some of my previous books. The first is a nonfiction book called *Become a Richer Writer*, the basic premise of which was to offer some suggestions to get a stalled writing career moving again. Every writer at one time or another thinks his or her career is not progressing fast enough. This book was a collection of remedies to give a seemingly flagging career a boost.

Here are a few of the idea cards that I generated. I'll only list six of them (the book's finished table of contents listed 31 chapters), and they are presented in no particular form or sequence.

Get Inspired
- The guys I used to play tennis with always played better during Wimbledon week. They got inspired by watching the best in the world play there.
- Read good writing.
- Read biographies or articles about good writers.
- Visit places where your heroes lived and worked.
- Visit places you're interested in.

Keep Improving
- Whatever you learn about writing, you must practice. It's the same in sports.
- Analyze your "Game":
  > John Wooden won many championships with different players because he used their individual talents to produce the best team.
- Find exercises to help you improve:
  > John Wooden, again, ran drills to help his players perfect certain skills.
  > Find exercises that will perfect your outstanding skills.
  > Find exercises that will eliminate certain flaws in your writing.
- Set aside time for improvement:
  > Add to your writing time: early in the morning; late at night.
  > Combine your practice with your normal activities.
  > Reevaluate and rearrange your writing-time budget.
  > Use "unusable" time:
    – Tell about a friend who learned a second language by studying it during his daily walks.

It's Your Career
- You must take charge of it and accept responsibility:
  > Decide on your own goal.
  > Be willing to pay the price to reach that goal.

> Take steps to achieve your goal.
> Do the work yourself, because:
  – Others are too busy.
  – Others are unreliable.
  – Others have no real stake in your career.

Analyze Your Past Writing for Ideas

- Recapture the enthusiasm you had when you wrote an excellent piece
- Be aware of what you did better in the past
- Notice how you've improved and capitalize on that
- Look INSIDE your writing for fresh adventures
  > Find different ideas within past pieces you've written
- Look OUTSIDE your writing for fresh adventures
  > Try a form of writing you've never attempted before

Demote Yourself

- Occasionally do some of those things that you feel you've outgrown or are too accomplished to attempt
  > They can broaden your outlook
    – Tell of the TV executive who was flying from New York to Los Angeles, looked out the window during the flight and said, "I never knew there were people down there."
  > They get you out of your "cloister."
  > They can expand your universe:
    – Meet new people in different professions.

Take Some Risks

- Shakespeare said, "We often lose the good we oft might win by fearing to attempt." Try something you've been fearful of.
- Maybe your career is stalled because you're intimidated by the next level. Give the next level a try.
- Occasionally break a traditional writing rule. See what happens.

When I got all 31 chapters laid out before me, it became apparent that the ideas fell into three distinct categories: ideas that had to do with the writer personally, ideas that had to do with actual writing, and ideas that had to do with selling that writing. Therefore, I split the book into three sections entitled "Part I—Look to Yourself," "Part II—Look to Your Writing," and "Part III—Look to Your Marketing." The cards titled **"Get Inspired," "It's**

Your Career," and **"Take Some Risks"** were included under Part I. **"Keep Improving"** and **"Analyze Your Past Writing for Ideas"** were listed under Part II. The card **"Demote Yourself"** became a chapter in Part III. Because the chapters were on separate index cards, it was easy to place them in the different categories.

As another example, I had contracted to write a book of jokes for children called *Super Funny School Jokes*. It would include about 400 separate gags suitable for youngsters and relating to school. Even though it was purely a listing of jokes, I still had to come up with things I could joke about—in other words, *ideas I wanted to talk about.*

Following are the ideas that I selected:

1. The First Day of School
2. What I Did During the Summer
3. Where Do They Go? (This chapter may need an explanation. It was a series of "Where do they go to school" jokes such as, "Where do prisoners go to college? Penn." "Where do snakes go to college? Pitt." You get the idea.)
4. Teachers I Have Known & Annoyed
5. Homework & Other Things I Don't Do
6. Tests Are Ruining My Grades
7. So Many Subjects—So Little Time
8. Making the Grades
9. These Books Are Not for Reading
10. Time Out
11. Kooky Classmates
12. Breaking the Dress Code
13. The School Cafeteria
14. Late Again!
15. Getting into Trouble
16. The Last Day of School

Here again, you can see the value of breaking an assignment up into bite-sized chunks. It's almost impossible to write 400 jokes about school. However, it is possible to write just a few jokes about the first day of school, a few about the school cafeteria, and some about being late, and then a few more about the last day of school. Assemble them and you have a volume of jokes about school. Once again, though, because the topics were isolated on individual index cards, I could arrange and re-arrange them until I arrived at the presentation order I felt worked best.

Does this concept of recording ideas in bite-sized chunks apply equally as well to fiction writing? Yes. In fact, in some instances, it works even better. You still must begin with a basic description of your story. With fiction, *what you want to say* becomes the different ideas you try to get across to the reader in each scene or chapter. So again, you chip away at the project. You plan as many scenes as you can, convert them to cards, and you start to lay out the entire storyboard. It may work better because you can see where new plot points are essential. You can also see that if you require conflict or problems in a scene later in the story, you can go back and plan for those earlier in the story. You get a fuller picture of the entire tale and can make adjustments where required.

For example, let's begin to create a simple book right now that we might write. It's about two sixth-graders who are bitter rivals, always trying to outdo one another. They are Eugene McGonigle, the narrator, and Eddie Melrick, the near perfect student who is admired and respected by all the school's teachers. We might begin by just getting one idea down on paper with a few supporting notes.

1ˢᵗ note: *Class Competition Day: Establish that this is an important day at this school. It's a day of several competitions, involving both sports and academic contests. The ending of the day is The School Essay Contest. The Overall Champion will be awarded a $100 prize.*

That's a start. It introduces an important element of conflict between our two main characters. Now we need more to support it

2ⁿᵈ note: *The Crooked Race: Eugene and Eddie are known to be the fastest kids in the school. One or the other is a shoo-in to win this race. Eugene's best friend, Rich Bulgar, secretly arranges for Eddie to be knocked out of the race. He kind of gives Eugene a sign that everything has been arranged. During the race a friend of Rich's "accidentally" gets tangled up with Eddie. They both tumble and are eliminated from the race. Eugene wins.*

3ʳᵈ note: *The Wrong Speech: As the contestants are preparing for the Essay Contest, Eugene discovers that he brought his homework assignment and not the essay he had diligently prepared for the competition. He asks his dad, who is there to watch the Essay Contest Competition, to go home and retrieve the speech. His dad does, but they're not sure Eugene will get the speech in time for his slot in the contest.*

4ᵗʰ note: *The Wrong Time Slot: The contestants pick their positions in the essay contest. Unfortunately, Eugene selects slot #2. There's no way he will have his speech by then. He's virtually eliminated.*

5th note: *The Switch: Again, Rich Bulgar steps in and arranges for Eugene to offer up his #2 slot to Eddie Melrick in exchange for the slot he pulled, #10. Eddie knows he's being conned, but he accepts the trade. He tells Eugene, "I want you in the contest because I want to beat you."*

6th note: *Eugene wins: Eddie does great as the 2nd speaker, but Eugene wins the contest. Eugene is grateful to Eddie and says, "How can I ever repay you?" Eddie says, "Let's run the race again. Just you and I. No other legs to trip over."*

OK. That's a basic plot outline. But as we lay it out, we can see that there are spaces that must be filled in. For example:

- We should establish the importance of the Class Competition Day and determine how we will present this.
- We should build up the rivalry between Eugene and Eddie. How did it get started? Maybe they're both vying for the same young girl's attention.
- How did Rich Bulgar and Eugene become best friends?
- We should have some scenes that show how devious Rich can be.
- We should know more about Eddie's character and personality, too.
- We must determine how the book will end. Does Eddie win the race? Does Eugene then forfeit his prize? Does Eugene win the race? Does it mean more to him having won it "fair and square?"
- We should establish that the two final competitions, the race and the essay contest, will be the deciding factors in who wins the overall trophy and the cash prize.

You can see that this process requires much further thought and planning in order to build a complete, viable story line. However, the program operates for both fiction and nonfiction book projects in the same way, by working on the project one bite-sized chunk at a time.

◆ ◆ ◆

Once you've completed the exercises in this chapter, give yourself a pat on the back. Your book is now more than a concept—it's become something tangible, and you've taken a critical early step in completing it. The next step in the program is to analyze and organize all of these ideas you've captured into a structure for your book.

CHAPTER 6

REFINE AND ORGANIZE YOUR LIST OF CHAPTERS

At this point of the program, you should have a compilation of all the things you would like to say in your book. In effect, this is your list of potential chapters. You've jotted them down in no particular form or sequence. You simply noted the ideas as they occurred to you. Now, the time has come to study and analyze your list and to begin to put it into a logical form, a form that will eventually become the full outline of your book—your table of contents.

In order to illustrate this process, let me begin by showing you the random list of chapter ideas I generated for my book *Comedy Writing Step by Step*. I will number them here to make it easier to reference them as we progress; however, keep in mind that these are in no particular order—at the moment. Secondly, since the accompanying notes I jotted down for each chapter are cryptic and have meaning only to me, I'll omit them from the listing. Just assume that as I listed the items I wanted to develop in this book I also made a few notes or reminders relating to those items. You should have done the same, as was discussed in Chapter 10. Your list might be briefer than mine; it could also be substantially longer. All that matters is that you went through the exercise in the previous chapter and generated a set of ideas that are candidates for being chapters in your book.

Here's the list we'll use as an example:

1. Comedy can be taught; it can be learned
2. *You* can write comedy

3. A collection of comedy writing exercises
4. Comedy can be a hobby, provide a second income, or become a professional career
5. You can teach yourself to write comedy by reading and listening to comedy and by actually going through the writing process
6. Keep a comedy notebook of ideas to write about or to use as references
7. Use factual statements to generate joke ideas
8. Ask questions to generate joke ideas
9. Exaggerate and distort to generate joke ideas
10. Use common sayings and expressions to generate joke ideas
11. Create formula jokes
12. Concepts that can add to the "funniness" of jokes you write
13. The value of writing complete monologues
14. Proper attitudes for beginning a comedy writing career
15. Tips on marketing the material you write
16. Allow the audience to finish the jokes
17. Writing "insult" humor without offending
18. The skills you'll need to acquire or develop to write comedy
19. Writing material on speculation
20. Proper preparation before beginning to write
21. Getting a career started
22. Practicing your trade
23. Keep your audience in mind when writing your jokes

That's the list that I had before me (each on separate index cards) as I began to organize the flow of the chapters. Now you're ready to manipulate, rearrange, and refine your own list into a logical sequence that will form the outline for your writing.

As I mentioned earlier, I recommend writing each idea on a separate index card. That way you can pin the cards onto a bulletin board and rearrange them with little trouble. Or, you can simply place them on a tabletop or desktop where you can easily reposition them. Also, you might have them arranged on a computer file where you can drag and drop them easily. Again, the specific procedure you use for manipulating your list of ideas is entirely up to you. The important thing is to get your random ideas into a visible form—one that you can manipulate and rearrange so that you can organize them into a book outline.

(**Author's note:** In order to get the most value out of this chapter, I suggest that you do that right now with the above sample list of my chapter headings. Jot each heading on a separate index card or a Post-it, so that you can physically rearrange them as you follow the rest of this chapter. If you prefer, you can type them into a computer list that you can rearrange with the drag-and-drop procedure. It will make the rest of this chapter easier to visualize and follow.)

DIVIDE CHAPTER HEADINGS INTO CATEGORIES

The first step in organizing your chapter headings is to try to identify separate major categories that they might fit into. A good example of this would be the process of writing a cookbook. Presumably, you would have several different types of recipes. They would readily fit into categories such as "Appetizers," "Salads," "Main Courses," and "Desserts." Now your cookbook has a structure and a flow to it. You would place each recipe into the appropriate category. The meat dishes would be placed in the "Main Courses" section; the cakes and pies would be separated into the "Desserts" section; and so on.

Suppose, though, you were writing a cookbook devoted exclusively to desserts. Those recipes would still fit into distinct categories, possibly "Pies," "Cakes," "Cookies," Puddings," and so on.

Sometimes the chapter headings you assemble won't fit into obvious categories as easily as recipes do, but with some analysis and investigation, you should be able to divide your book into discrete sections. Let's again refer to the chapter headings that I listed for *Comedy Writing Step by Step* earlier in this chapter. I noticed when I assembled them that some of the headings had nothing to do with the actual writing of comedy. Several of the proposed chapters were almost pep talks that were designed to inspire the readers to at least try comedy writing. A couple of them discussed certain skills that the reader should develop or acquire to become a comedy writer. Then there was a chapter discussing the various career-related facets of comedy writing: hobby, second income, or full-time profession.

So I divided the book into three parts. Part One I labeled "Deciding to Write." Part Two I called "Building Your Skills." Part Three I named "Building Your Career." (**Author's note:** Now you'll need additional index cards or Post-its or computer titles for the Part One, Part Two, and Part Three sections of the book.)

If you glance back over that list of chapter headings above, you'll notice that the items

1. Comedy writing can be taught; it can be learned

2. *You* can write comedy
4. Comedy writing can be a hobby, provide a second income, or become a professional career
18. The skills you'll need to acquire or develop to write comedy

fall under the heading of "Deciding to Write." I included them in Part One.

Item 5 ("You can teach yourself to write comedy by reading and listening to comedy and by actually going through the writing process") might have also been included in this group, but it seemed to me that it was better suited for "Part Two—Building Your Skills," because it dealt primarily with *learning* to write comedy. You, as the author, will need to make similar judgments in positioning the chapters in your book. Often, it is simply a seat-of-the-pants decision.

Under "Part Two—Building Your Skills," I included the chapters that deal with the actual writing of material:

3. A collection of comedy writing exercises
5. You can teach yourself to write comedy by reading and listening to comedy and by actually going through the writing process (we discussed this item above)
6. Keep a comedy notebook of ideas to write about or to use as references
7. Use factual statements to generate joke ideas
8. Ask questions to generate joke ideas
9. Exaggerate and distort to generate joke ideas
10. Use common sayings and expressions to generate joke ideas
11. Create formula jokes
12. Concepts that can add to the "funniness" of jokes you write
13. The value of writing complete monologues
16. Allow the audience to finish the jokes
17. Writing "insult" humor without offending
20. Proper preparation before beginning to write
23. Keep your audience in mind when writing your jokes

"Part Three—Building Your Career" included items that all had to do with developing a career or marketing material:

14. Proper attitudes for beginning a comedy writing career
15. Tips on marketing the material you write
19. Writing material on speculation

21. Getting a career started
22. Practicing your trade

It's not essential that you divide every book into segments. Some books don't lend themselves to that sort of division, and with other manuscripts it may be more bothersome and distracting than it is worthwhile. In Chapter 10, for example, I listed a series of chapter headings for my book *Super Funny School Jokes*. To me, there was no point in breaking those into segments. They were all about school, so they all fit into one category. Nevertheless, it is worth examining your collection of chapter headings to see if you can find a reasonable division. Good categorization can make the book easier to read. Going back to our example of the cookbook, you can imagine how confusing it would be to have a collection of recipes that were in no logical order and were not divided into categories.

ARRANGE YOUR CHAPTER HEADINGS INTO A LOGICAL SEQUENCE

Now that you've got your chapter headings divided into categories, some important work still remains in shaping your book: You now must arrange those chapters within each category into a logical sequence. Doing this not only makes the book easier to read, but for you, the author, it makes it easier to write. When one chapter naturally leads into another chapter, both the writing and the reading flow much more smoothly.

Let's take a look at Part One of my example. It now lists items 1, 2, 4, and 18, which would mean the chapter headings for that section of the book are as follows:

1. Comedy writing can be taught; it can be learned
2. *You* can write comedy
4. Comedy writing can be a hobby, provide a second income, or become a professional career
18. The skills you'll need to acquire or develop to write comedy

Because I felt it was critical to get across to the readers the fact that *they* can write comedy, it was clear that a more logical sequence for Part One would be to begin with Chapter 2, and then discuss the idea that comedy writing could be learned and taught. Therefore, I rearranged the cards for those chapters and moved Chapter 2 ahead of Chapter 1.

(AUTHOR'S NOTE: Just a reminder. I hope you're actually laying out the cards, Post-Its, or using your computer skills to rearrange chapters as we go. If you are, move the cards accordingly now…and, of course, move them as we continue with this example.)

Also, I felt that after telling the readers that they could learn comedy, it would make sense to tell them what skills they should develop or acquire. Then together we could investigate the different options of comedy writing: hobby, second income, or professional career. So I switched the last two chapter headings of this section by moving Chapter 18 ahead of Chapter 4.

With this new arrangement, I was telling the readers (1) that comedy writing was available to them, (2) if they didn't have the skills now, they could learn them, (3) what specific skills they would have to develop or acquire, and (4) that they could enjoy comedy writing at any one of three different levels (hobby, second income, or professional career). It seemed to me that this section of the book now flowed in an understandable and logical order.

I followed similar reasoning in rearranging the other two sections of the book. Rather than go through the thinking process and the rearranging with you, I'll simply list the new order for the chapters below. (AUTHOR's NOTE: I renumbered the chapter headings for this revised, finalized listing, and the new numbers will be referred to from this point on in the chapter. I suggest that you rearrange your index cards, Post-its, or computer listings to reflect the following arrangement. If you had the original numbers on your list, it would be a good idea to change them now to the new numbers. Just cross out the old number, and jot the new one in.)

Part One—Deciding to Write

1. *You* can write comedy
2. Comedy writing can be taught; it can be learned
3. The skills you'll need to acquire or develop to write comedy
4. Comedy writing can be a hobby, provide a second income, or become a professional career

Part Two—Building Your Skills

5. You can teach yourself to write comedy by reading and listening to comedy and by actually going through the writing process
6. A collection of comedy writing exercises
7. The value of writing complete monologues
8. Proper preparation before beginning to write
9. Use factual statements to generate joke ideas
10. Ask questions to generate joke ideas
11. Exaggerate and distort to generate joke ideas

12. Use common sayings and expressions to generate joke ideas
13. Create formula jokes
14. Concepts that can add to the "funniness" of jokes you write
15. Keep your audience in mind when writing your jokes
16. Allow the audience to finish the jokes
17. Writing "insult" humor without offending
18. Keep a comedy notebook of ideas to write about or to use as references

Part Three—Building Your Career

19. Proper attitudes for beginning a comedy writing career
20. Getting a career started
21. Practicing your trade
22. Writing material on speculation
23. Tips on marketing the material you write

At this stage, you should have listed all of the things you want to say in your book (those have become your chapter headings), and you have arranged them in a logical flow to form a basic outline for your writing. However, you still have some chores remaining in this part of the program. Remember, I warned you earlier that starting and completing a book is not an easy task. It requires considerable *Organization*. The work we're doing now is part of that organizing. I also cautioned you that finishing a book would require *Discipline*. Part of the discipline is that you must stick with this phase of the organizing until you have an outline that can guide you through the writing and the completion of your book.

Now that you have the outline (to this point) before you, you may want to revise it even further—to combine, separate, or delete certain chapter headings.

COMBINE CHAPTER HEADINGS

Earlier, I urged you to simply jot down ideas that you wanted to cover in your book. This was a brainstorming task. You put your thoughts on paper without concerning yourself with form, sequence, or much else, for that matter. You were focused on just getting your ideas captured for future reference. Now that you have them captured and better organized, you want to refine them. It's possible that you may have been too ambitious in jotting down some of those ideas. Some may not support a full chapter. That's fine. Now is the time to either combine them with other chapters or simply give them a mention in a broader chapter.

To illustrate, if you look at items 9 through 13 in the above listing, you'll recognize that they all refer to various ways of generating joke ideas. They can all be included in a single chapter that deals with "Ways of Getting the Joke Ideas Flowing." Can similar adjustments be made with your list of ideas?

DIVIDE IDEAS INTO SEPARATE CHAPTER HEADINGS

Some of the ideas you've included may be larger than you envisioned. Rather than group them into one chapter, you might consider devoting a separate chapter to each specific idea. For instance, in the sample listing above, item 4 includes three areas of comedy writing: hobby, second income, or professional career. When I reached this point of my planning, I decided that I could devote a full chapter to each. So where I had one index card representing a chapter entitled "Comedy writing can be a hobby, a second income, or a professional career," I now had three index cards with chapters entitled "Comedy writing as a hobby," "Comedy writing as a second income," and "Comedy writing as a professional career." You'll see that reflected in the final outline of the book, to follow. (You should add those new chapters into your mockup, too.)

DELETE CHAPTER HEADINGS

My program earlier urged you to be almost promiscuous in getting ideas committed to paper. Consequently, you may now decide that some of your chapter headings are unnecessary or inappropriate for this book. If so, remove them.

Using our sample listing again, I decided that items 16 and 17 might be too advanced for this volume. They could be more beneficial in a follow-up book that goes into more specifics about comedy writing. So, I removed them from the list.

It's also possible that in generating the various ideas for your book, you might inadvertently list the same idea under two different headings. For instance, you might have a chapter titled, "Getting your material to the market place," and another one titled, "Marketing your material." They're virtually the same idea. So, you might want to search out and delete those chapters that are duplicates.

Take a good look at your list; is there anything that doesn't seem to be a good fit?

FILL HOLES IN THE LOGICAL SEQUENCE

One benefit of having the entire book laid out in sequence is that you can more easily notice omissions. As you review your step–by-step progression, you may notice that certain steps or topics are missing. Now is the time to add such items, before you begin the actual writing.

Again, using my outline as an example, you'll notice that item 7 promotes the value of writing a complete monologue. The next item then discusses preparing to write. There is no chapter that guides the reader in forming a complete monologue. Therefore, I added a new chapter heading about "Routining Jokes into a Monologue." Now, the text not only advises readers to write complete monologues, but it also gives them instructions on how to accomplish that.

NEW CHAPTERS

It's possible that in seeing the entire manuscript outline, you decide that you haven't included all the things you wanted to say on your topic. This is the proper time to correct those omissions.

In my book outline, I dealt mostly with writing one-liners because I considered that form the basic building block of humor. I did have a chapter that explained this concept and mentioned that if one could master this joke form, he or she could graduate to other longer forms of comedy writing. However, after looking at the outline, I felt that I should at least touch on certain of those longer forms, so I added two chapters, one on "Sketch Writing" and one on "Sitcom Writing."

Even then, I felt that there might have been other areas of writing that weren't touched upon. To compensate for this, I added an appendix to the outline. This was a section that included answers to most of the questions I had heard from beginning writers about the craft of comedy writing. (Add these new chapter headings to your mockup.)

Now, at last, the book outline was complete. By now, you're probably sick of seeing and hearing about it, but I'll take the risk of listing the final version here for your reference:

Part One—Deciding to Write

1. *You* can write comedy
2. Comedy writing can be taught; it can be learned
3. The skills you'll need to acquire or develop to write comedy
4. Comedy writing as a hobby

5. Comedy writing as a second income
6. Comedy writing as a professional career

Part Two—Building Your Skills

7. You can teach yourself to write comedy by reading and listening to comedy and by actually going through the writing process
8. A collection of comedy writing exercises
9. The value of writing complete monologues
10. Proper preparation before beginning to write
11. Methods for getting the jokes flowing
12. Routining jokes into a monologue
13. Concepts that can add to the "funniness" of jokes you write
14. Keep your audience in mind when writing your jokes
15. Keep a comedy notebook of ideas to write about or to use as references
16. Sketch writing
17. Sitcom writing

Part Three—Building Your Career

18. Proper attitudes for beginning a comedy writing career
19. Getting a career started
20. Practicing your trade
21. Writing material on speculation
22. Tips on marketing the material you write
23. Appendix: questions and answers about comedy writing

Your book outline should be at least this complete and this detailed. Let's quickly review the steps that you followed to arrive at this point:

1. You made a comprehensive list of those things you want to say in your book.
   a. You noted a few reminders in the process.
   b. There was no particular order (simply brainstorming ideas).
2. You transferred your ideas to a form that you could easily rearrange.
   a. Index cards
   b. Post-Its
   c. Computer files that you can cut and paste
3. You looked for natural divisions of these ideas in order to break your book into logical subdivisions (Part I, Part II, or something similar).

4. You filed the various items (or chapters) under the separate divisions of your book.
5. You arranged all of the chapters into a logical sequence.
6. You refined the outline further by doing the following:
   a. Combining items into one chapter
   b. Dividing items into separate chapters
   c. Deleting chapters (for whatever reasons)
   d. Adding new chapters to fill holes in the logical sequence
   e. Adding new chapters because you may have overlooked them earlier and now feel they are necessary

Remember that this is not a process that you will likely complete in one day or even in one week. It takes time and focus. Concentrate on each item as you're jotting down those thoughts you want to include, then focus on the overall outline as you rearrange it and refine it. This is the outline that you'll use in generating the text. If it's designed well, it will be a big help in completing that task.

Here are some of the benefits of producing a detailed, definitive outline of your entire project:

1. You can now envision your entire book with increased clarity. With the full manuscript laid out before you, you can more readily and effectively evaluate it. Is it comprehensive? Does it cover and explain all the ideas that you wanted to convey to your reader? Are there questions that are left unanswered? Now is the time to correct any flaws you spot in your outline. Keep in mind that none of these preparatory steps are immutable. Your book is not finished until it's finished. You can change it at any point in the process. It is easier, though, to make the changes before beginning to write the text rather than afterward.
2. You have given in-depth thought to your entire book.
   a. This is much easier than trying to create form and structure as you write. Like a contractor who depends on detailed blueprints in order to construct a house to specifications, you depend on your outline to write your book the way it deserves to be written and should be written.
   b. Following a well-designed outline keeps you on track as you write. Without a plan, it's easy to slide off onto tangents. If you do, the book you're writing can become totally different from the one you

intended to write. Should you go too far afield, it's often difficult to rewrite yourself back to your original book idea.

3. You have notes to guide you in the writing of each chapter. Remember, the program suggested that as you record the things you want to say, you support them with key word notes to remind you of what you have in mind for this chapter. Consequently, you avoid beginning each chapter "cold."

4. The plan allows you, if you choose, to write out of sequence. Because your overall plan guarantees that all the pieces fit, you can work on chapters in any order without destroying the continuity of your writing. Of course, there's nothing wrong with beginning your writing with Chapter 1 and continuing on to the conclusion. However, here are a few possible reasons why *being able* to write out of sequence could be beneficial.

   a. You may have a limited block of time to devote to a particular writing session. In that case, you might select a chapter that won't require more time than you have. You can start and complete a chapter, even though it's out of sequence.

   b. You may be faced with a particularly challenging chapter. It could even be one that intimidates you. Sometimes, such chapters can threaten your momentum. By being able to write out of sequence, you can attack this menacing chapter early and get it out of your way. This could be the morale boost you need to attack the rest of the project with renewed enthusiasm.

   c. Writing out of sequence can also permit you to "chip away" at certain chapters. As an example, in one of my books I had a chapter that included 101 different projects that the reader could try. It's difficult in one writing session to create 101 different ideas. However, since I knew this chapter was planned in the book and where it was positioned, I could use any free writing time I had to generate just a few ideas that could be included in this chapter. After ten short sessions of generating ten ideas at a time, I practically had the entire chapter written.

5. The overall plan helps you eliminate duplication. Because you have your chapters planned out and each one is well-defined, you should know exactly which points you'll cover in each. Writing without a plan, it's quite easy to repeat in Chapter 6 what you've already explained in Chapter 2. Avoiding duplication of text and ideas will

make your completed first draft much more coherent and the rewriting of your text that much easier.

6. A complete and comprehensive plan helps avoid inadvertent contradictions. It's easy sometimes to make a statement early in the manuscript and then contradict it later. With the entire concept in front of you, it's much easier to avoid such flaws. Also, though, you may make certain statements that *could appear* to be contradictions. Knowing where such instances may occur in your manuscript, you can be ready to explain why the seeming contradiction is not a contradiction at all.

SOME ADVICE ON CHAPTER TITLES

Congratulations! In a sense, you've now virtually written your entire book. All that remains is to add the words (no small task!). We'll get started on that in the next chapter. However, before we move on, let's cover a few more details about your outline and your chapter headings.

While we're on the subject of your chapter headings, I'd like to offer a few more suggestions. The outline you have generated is pretty much the table of contents for your book. Many potential book buyers glance through the table of contents when deciding whether to purchase a book or not. Most will look at the front cover, read the back cover, take a quick look at the table of contents, and then maybe scan a page or two before buying the book. Publishers and agents also will carefully inspect your table of contents. So spicing up the table of contents could help in selling your book —both to the publisher and eventually to the buying public once it reaches the bookstore shelves.

One way to promote your book is to write enticing, intriguing, clever chapter titles. For example, you could create intentionally cryptic chapter titles that make the reader want to see exactly what you're talking about. Captivate the reader with the title and let the text explain the meaning. A colleague of mine, Bob Mills, wrote a book about the Bob Hope writers (*The Laugh Makers*, Bear Manor Media, 2009). Here are a few chapter titles:

- Running Naked through the Lobby
- Laying 1000-Year-Old Eggs
- Saluting the Clown at Jack-in-the-Box

Honestly, don't they make you want to read the chapters to find out what those intriguing titles signify? Each one of them is explained in the text, but you have to pick up the book and read it to find out. Not a bad device, huh?

I've also seen books that have a quotation acting as a subtitle to each chapter heading. It's always a quote that has some reference to the main premise of the chapter and always from some well-known figure. It adds credibility to whatever you say in your text to indicate right at the start that Benjamin Franklin (or whomever) agrees with you.

I used this device in the title pages for the different parts of the book we've been using as an example in this chapter, *Comedy Writing Step by Step.* The quote for PART ONE—DECIDING TO WRITE reads:

> *What I want to do is make people laugh so they'll see things seriously.*
> —WILLIAM R. ZINSER

The selection included in PART TWO—BUILDING YOUR SKILLS was:

> *If the desire to write is not accompanied by actual writing,*
> *then the desire is not to write.*
> —HUGH PRATHER

PART THREE—BUILDING YOUR CAREER featured a longer quote:

> *Nothing in the world can take the place of perseverance.*
> *Talent will not; nothing in the world is more common than men*
> *with talent. Genius will not; unrewarded genius is almost a proverb.*
> *Education will not; the world is full of educated derelicts.*
> *Perseverance and determination alone are omnipotent.*
> *The slogan "Press On" has solved and always will solve*
> *the problems of the human race.*
> —CALVIN COOLIDGE

Another device that may help spice up your table of contents is to include a brief synopsis with each chapter heading. In just a few short words, tell the reader what the chapter will deliver. Make a promise to the reader. Again, if those potential buyers who glance through the table of contents see something in there that looks appealing, it could mean another sale for your book.

CHAPTER 7

DESCRIBE EACH OF YOUR CHAPTERS

LET'S REVIEW WHAT YOU'VE ACCOMPLISHED so far with this program:

1. You've selected which book you intend to write. Of course, you probably already had a project in mind which is why you decided to read this book in the first place.

2. You've established that the idea you have in mind is substantial enough to produce a complete book. You've written a brief description of the book you intend to complete. The details of this step were covered in Chapter 4 (DEFINE YOUR BOOK).

3. You began to chip away at the development of your project by noting the various topics you want to cover in your book. This was a brainstorming project that noted all those concepts you felt should be included in your book—in no particular order or sequence. You simply wanted to get them recorded. As you listed the various ideas, you included a few simple notes to support each item. Chapter 5 (START CHIPPING AWAY) discussed this process.

4. After your list was complete, you organized the topics into a logical sequence. In essence, you laid out the chapters of your book, perhaps even grouping these chapters into separate sections of your book. This work forms the blueprint for the *construction* of your manuscript. You can refer to Chapter 6 (REFINE AND ORGANIZE YOUR LIST OF CHAPTERS) to refresh your thinking on this step.

Again I'll remind you as you progress through this program that the above steps are not a one-day process. You should devote considerable time to each of them and be sure not to quit too soon. The more complete your planning process is, the easier it will be to finish a draft of your book. I generally allow myself anywhere from four to eight weeks to plan a book before beginning the actual writing of the text.

Now that you have a completed outline of your project, though, my program recommends getting even *more* specific before you begin writing the text. At this point in the program you should write a brief description of each of the chapters in your outline. The objective of this step is to record those points you want each chapter to convey. In other words, tell yourself what you intend to tell the readers. You have noted what you want to say and you've organized that into an intelligent sequence and format. Now you want to record the specific purpose for each of your chapters.

In this description you should, for each chapter:

1. Include and expand on any notes that you made earlier when you were simply jotting down those ideas you wanted to get across in this book.
2. Detail those elements you want this chapter to accomplish.
3. Note ways that you might convey those ideas to the reader:
   a. Anecdotes
   b. Appropriate quotes
   c. Examples
   d. Logic that supports your ideas.

You will go through each chapter one more time before you begin writing the text, but whatever thoughts you have now that will help you write each chapter in the future, should be included at this point.

By way of illustration, I'll list the chapter descriptions that I wrote when I was planning this book. I'll do a brief synopsis of the Introduction, Chapter 1, and Chapter 2. As I reprint them here, I'll include some notes that further explain my reasoning as I was composing them.

Introduction: What This Book Is and Is Not

This book has a front and back cover. You've probably read some or all of the back cover. That back cover is most important. Why? Because it means the book is finished. There are no more pages to come. There are no chapters to follow that back cover. Everything that I wanted to say and had to say has been said in the pages that are between the front and back covers.

The purpose of this book is to get you, your writing, and your project to that back cover—figuratively and literally.

(NOTE: This was my idea for the actual opening of the Introduction. It seemed like a good idea, so I included it here in my notes so that I wouldn't forget it when I did begin to write the copy. You can refer back to the actual copy in the Introduction of this volume to see how closely I followed this note.)

This is NOT a book on writing, creativity, style, or technique. It's a not a book to help you form characters or plot out a compelling story. There are other good books available that help you do that. This book assumes you're someone who wants to say something—either tell a story or convey valuable information. This book assumes you have a book of your own in your soul. Its intention is to help you get that book out of yourself, onto paper, and make it readable by others. How you write and what you write is of no concern to this volume. All it wants to do is get your book written.

This does not imply that writing style is not important. It is. However, the greatest writing in the world would be useless if it were left undone. Give examples of great book beginnings and what they would be like if the writers decided to postpone or abandon the writing.

Do learn to write and write well. Develop your particular style and unique writing voice, but above all, finish your book.

Describe then, what this book IS. It will get you started on your project. It will guide you in planning and organizing your writing. It will guide you through that process until you can say to yourself, "This book is complete."

That's a great moment.

(NOTE: Here again, I considered this a usable ending for this chapter. You can look back at the closing lines of the Introduction to see how closely I adhered to these notes.)

Chapter 1—So What's Keeping You From Writing Your Book?

In this chapter I will mention that the reason most books never get published is because they never get written in the first place. Then, I will list possible reasons why books never get completed. (I've assembled eight reasons and they are already listed in my notes for the writing classes I teach on *Starting and Finishing Your Book*.) With each reason I mention, I will also offer a solution.

(NOTE: I will not list those eight reasons here because they are included as part of this book in Chapter 1.)

Chapter 2—No One Can Write a Book

The purpose of this chapter is to outline the basic ideas for this book-completing system. I'll go through each phase of the procedure one at a time. I'll just touch on them in this chapter and then expand on each one as we get further into the text.

This chapter will first point out that it's impossible for anyone to *write a book*. Charles Dickens couldn't, Stephen King can't. J.K. Rowling can't. All any of them can do is write part of a book. Give examples of this. You can't eat an entire steak. That's why the restaurants furnish sharp steak knives, so you can carve the meat into bite-sized chunks. You eat only part of the porterhouse at a time. Eventually, you complete the entire delicious cut of beef.

That's how the book-writing process of this system works. You break the book down into bite-sized chunks.

Point out that a book can be overwhelming at first. Often the fear of that daunting task keeps the writer from even beginning.

HOWEVER, there is more to it than just writing one chunk at a time. The chunks must eventually blend together to form an understandable "whole." That's why a writing plan and schedule are required. Use a blueprint of a house as an analogy.

Then, of course, the writer must be disciplined enough to stick to his or her writing schedule.

THE PURPOSE OF THIS STEP

Writing out this full chapter–by-chapter outline will provide you with a fairly detailed road map for the writing of your book. You want to have a full overview of the writing that you'll be doing once you begin the manuscript.

THE BENEFITS OF THIS STEP

1. It helps maintain your writing momentum:
   a. Once you begin writing your book, you can continue your writing. You have each chapter laid out before you so you can proceed

almost without interruption. This is a tremendous benefit in *completing* your book.

b. It helps maintain your enthusiasm. At the beginning of your project, you're excited about the writing adventure. You have a book you want to write and you're eager to get going with it. However, if the momentum is destroyed, it can demoralize you. Constantly running into roadblocks can shake your confidence. It can influence you to abandon your book totally. However, having a well-planned road map can keep you going and help you maneuver around roadblocks. It smooths out the adventure enough so that you can remain excited about it.

c. It helps keep you on schedule. We'll discuss creating a workable schedule later in this book, but sticking to a schedule is an important facet of this program. It's essential to keep a fairly regular schedule in order to complete your manuscript. It's easier to stay on that schedule when you have the chapters planned. Otherwise, it would be like taking a road trip without laying out a route beforehand. Imagine if you had to drive a few blocks then pull over to see where you'll go next. Then once you drive a few more blocks, you have to stop and recheck the map. It would not only take forever to get where you're going, but it would be almost unbearable. Likewise, having a chapter–by-chapter plan for your book enables you to continue to work and complete various sections in a timely fashion and without stop-and-go annoyances.

d. It eliminates having to restart the writing process with each new chapter. Much of the thinking and planning for the individual chapters has already been done, so once you complete one chapter, you can attack the next one on the run. There's no inertia to overcome.

e. Because of all the above reasons, you should be able to write your book faster.

2. It triggers your memory:

a. We mentioned earlier that "no one can write a book." You can only write part of a book. By the same logic, none of us one can remember *everything* we want to include in our book. However, by jotting down the thoughts that we want to include in each chapter, there's no need to *remember* everything because we've made notes about everything. It's like keeping an address book. You can't possibly recall every single phone number you might want to call. However, you don't have to. They're all listed in your handy address book.

    b. You're more likely to include everything that you wanted to include in each chapter…and in a logical, coherent order.

    c. It makes it easier to establish the flow of each chapter because you've preplanned so much of it. You have all of the elements before you so you can more readily and more easily arrange them as you write. Suppose, for example, you have completed the writing of a certain chapter and then discover there is an element you wanted in that chapter, but forgot to include it. Going back to add it in can destroy the continuity of your writing. And, in fact, forcing it into the chapter now could require extensive, complicated rewriting.

3. You can write your chapters in any order:

    a. You have all you need to know to write any chapter with little fear of disrupting the other chapters.

    b. Should you opt to write your chapters in sequence, having a chapter-by-chapter plan is beneficial in that you are confident that you're including everything fully in each chapter.

    c. It helps continue your enthusiasm because you are free to write about whatever you feel like writing about at any particular time. If you're enthused about Chapter 10, for instance, you can write it. You have a complete overall plan so you know exactly what Chapter 10 should say.

    d. It frees your writing because you can dispatch troublesome chapters early and get them out of the way. Or, you can get a head start on your project by writing the easier chapters first. Whatever attack seems the most efficient is open to you because your overall plan is complete and allows you this freedom.

4. You can write each chapter practically free of interruption. You've already thought through not only the entire book, but each of the chapters. Therefore, as you write the chapter, there is little need to stop, think, plan, and start again.

5. It helps avoid duplication of concepts, examples, illustrations, anecdotes, quotes, or whatever. It's often easy to use an anecdote in Chapter 2 of your manuscript and then use it again when you get to Chapter 20 of your book. Sometimes you'll think to yourself, *I think I used that story before.* Now that means you'll have to page through the manuscript to try to find out if you used it before and, if you did,

where in the text it's located. It can be embarrassing if you don't catch the duplications, and even if you do catch them, it's time consuming to find them and replace one instance or the other. However, if you have already planned out which concepts, examples, illustrations, anecdotes, and quotes you'll use in each chapter, it makes avoiding duplications much easier.

Now you have your book completely outlined, chapter by chapter, and you're ready to write the book. But...how long will that process take? You don't really know because up until this point in the process you haven't written any text. You've simply written ideas, thoughts—mostly short, cryptic notes to yourself. Now you have to discover how long it will take you to convert those notes to the final text. Let's get started on that now.

CHAPTER 8

WRITE A CHAPTER

You have your complete book mapped out, along with a clear idea of what each chapter should accomplish. This is a good time to write one of those chapters. Get a feel right now for converting your ideas from the planning stage to the written text.

Select a chapter that you'd like to begin writing. It can be any chapter at all. It's probably a good idea to choose one that you're enthused about. Maybe pick a chapter that defines your overall book, one that sets the stage for what's to come. However, the choice is totally yours. Remember, this is *your* book. You write it anyway you like and in whatever order you prefer.

However, I'm going to make one further recommendation before you settle in front of your keyboard. We've spoken of FOCUS many times in this program. Now is a good time to utilize it. *Before beginning the actual writing of this chapter*, allow some time to think about what you're going to write and how you're going to write it. In other words, give this chapter time to "marinate." In fact, I recommend this practice for each of the chapters in your book. There are two parts to this chapter "marination" process. First, simply allow some time for the ideas in this chapter to *seep* into your mind. Writers seem to have that facility—even when we're not thinking about our writing, we're thinking about our writing. Allow some time for that to happen.

> Have you ever had someone's name escape your memory? This happens to me constantly. I'll be watching an old movie, and I see an actor I know well, but I can't recall the name. It can be annoying and distracting. Instead of enjoying the movie, I'm trying to think of who this guy is.

> When that happens, you struggle to recall that name. You try to almost physically extract it from you mind. However, nothing happens. Eventually, you abandon the effort. You relax. Then suddenly—seemingly from nowhere—that name pops clearly into your mind.
>
> That shows that even when you weren't thinking about it, you were thinking about it.
>
> It's not an unusual occurrence for writers. Many times my partner and I would wrestle with a particular writing problem. Then we'd take our lunch break, forget about the script completely, enjoy our food and discuss sports, the weather, or some other mundane topic. Then, over coffee, the solution we were searching for would pop into our heads— again seemingly out of nowhere.
>
> Though we thought we weren't thinking about our writing, we were.

Second, do think consciously about each chapter you're about to write. Focus on how you'll begin the chapter—how you'll you entice your reader into your text? Know what device you'll use to pique the reader's interest in what you're about to say? Maybe an anecdote would serve your purpose? How about a particularly appropriate quote? Do you have one? Can you find one? Maybe you should open with an example or an illustration that you'll explain more fully as you get further into the chapter. Would some interesting statistics attract the reader's curiosity? Think it through and formulate at least a few ideas for a captivating, intriguing opening paragraph or two.

Decide on what information you'll offer the readership in this chapter, and in what order you'll present it. Form a general outline of how you'll progress through the writing of this chapter.

Make notes of any research you have to do. You needn't stop to do the research while you're focusing on this chapter, but you should have a pretty good idea of what facts you'll need to establish to support your ideas in this part of the book. Be sure, though, to do all that research before you begin your writing. Then, when you get to that portion of your writing that demands statistics, you'll have them ready and can type them in without interrupting your writing. This will allow you to maintain your momentum. The American humorist, Don Marquis, may have been kidding when he said, "I never think when I write. Nobody can do two things at once and do them well." Nevertheless, his quip makes a point—get your research done before you start typing, so it doesn't interrupt your writing flow.

Suppose, for example, you want to make several points in your chapter and also offer examples to illustrate them. Collect those examples now. In fact, it's a good idea to gather a few more than you'll need. That way, you can pick the optimum one or two when you get to that point in your writing.

Assure yourself that you've included everything you want to convey in your chapter. Reread the original notes you made when you were deciding what you wanted to say in your book. Reread the synopsis you wrote on this chapter. There may be a few notes in those reminders that you've overlooked. If there are, find out where they should be placed in this current outline.

When you're convinced that your thoughts for this chapter are comprehensive and well-supported, decide how you'll close the chapter. Will you restate the premise? Will you add a seductive line that leads the reader into the following chapter? Think it through and prepare a plan of attack for your last few sentences.

In other words, FOCUS on your selected chapter, and on that chapter alone. Again, as was stipulated earlier in this program, no one can write a book—one can only write part of a book.

Now you're ready to turn on your computer and start writing the chapter you've outlined. The following are some recommendations for you to keep in mind as you do this:

TAKE YOUR TIME

Finally, you've begun writing the text. The inclination now is to get to the end so you can package the manuscript and get it into publication. It seems as soon as we start writing, we writers tend to want to finish our writing; most writers would rather *have written* than *have to write*. Now that you've started your text, you're eager to complete it.

The wiser course—one which generally produces more interesting and more readable writing—is to take your time. Enjoy the process. Writing this book—no, let's change that—writing this chapter should be fun for you. The more enjoyable it is for you, the more fun it likely will be for the reader.

Rushing through the text can produce a very "thin" manuscript. The feeling the reader gets from it is that the author said, "Here's what I have to say. I've said it. So there, it's done." It can be unsatisfying.

By taking time with your project and contemplating all of the items it contains, you will produce a much fuller manuscript. By "fuller," I don't mean that it's necessarily a bigger or longer volume, but that the ideas in it are explored thoroughly. This applies in both nonfiction and fiction.

Any ideas you present in nonfiction should be developed in some depth. Where did the idea come from? When was it first introduced? Who created it? Who else supports it? Are there quotes that corroborate it? Are there examples that more fully explain it? Are there anecdotes that bring it alive? Are there benefits that accrue from following the advice? Are there instructions that the reader can follow in order to use these ideas?

In short, you don't want to simply offer a fact and then move on. You and your reader will enjoy the fact more if it is offered with some dimensions to give it substance.

Similarly, plot developments in fiction should be offered with some foundation to them. It creates very unsatisfying reading to simply say that such and such a person takes such and such an action and then ask the reader to accept that. It's much more fulfilling to tell why such and such a person was faced with such and such a decision. What in the person's background might influence his or her decision? What other people or events might have a bearing on this particular decision? What other choices might have been available? What might be the results of the various other choices?

In other words, the reader doesn't want to know simply what happened, but also why it happened, what else might have happened, and so on. Offer a full, broad vista of each event so the reader not only has a better understanding of the story, but also a more enjoyable reading of it.

Let the reader know not only where the character in the story is, but what it *feels* like to be there. Let your audience know what the character feels, what the character sees, what the character tastes and smells, what sounds that character hears. Let the reader be there, too, and experience all the sensations with the character.

This idea ties in pretty closely with the next writing recommendation....

CONVERSE WITH YOUR READERS

As you know, my background is in writing and teaching comedy. In working with aspiring comedians, I emphasize that comedy is not simply standing at a microphone with pages and pages of solid jokes. If those factors were the only ones involved, stand-up comedy would be unbearably dull. The blasting cap that makes it explode into a glorious event of fun is . . . the audience. Comedy is only fun if it generates laughter. Laughter comes from the people sitting out front. So I emphasize that comedy entertainers should acknowledge and tailor their acts to those people. I suggest that rather than recite jokes—even solid gags—the comedian *converse* with the audience. Become a part of the audience. Not only offer them fun, but have fun along with them. Invite them to have fun along with you.

The same should apply to your writing. There would be no incentive and it would be senseless to write a book if you knew that no one would ever read it. As an author, you need an audience as much as a comedian needs one. There are readers out there. You are writing for them. Become a part of your own readership. Write your book as if you were having a face-to-face conversation with your readers. Write your book as if you were in a living room with a small gathering of them and you were telling your story in that intimate setting. Try to make your book read like a pleasant chat, rather than like an insurance policy or a police report.

Nevertheless, you still have information to convey. That leads us to the next writing recommendation….

BE SURE YOU *EXPLAIN* EVERYTHING TO YOUR READERS

Indulge me once again and let me refer back to comedy to illustrate this point. As a speaker, I often tell a story about my first military jaunt with Bob Hope. It was a Christmas Special that we taped for the troops fighting in Beirut, Lebanon. We did our shows on ships stationed just off the coast of Beirut.

The USO sponsored our trip and gave each of us in the Bob Hope troupe a white satin tennis jacket with an emblem on the breast, and on the back there was a large caricature of Bob Hope and red, white, and blue lettering that said, "Bob Hope USO Tour—Beirut, Lebanon." I wore this jacket everywhere on the trip. One time, a marine came over to me and asked if he could have his picture taken with me. I, of course, agreed. He went to give the camera to a marine buddy of his to snap the picture. When this marine came back to me, I gave him my biggest smile and put my arm around his shoulder. This was Christmas Eve in 1982, but to this day, I'll never forget what he said to me. He said, "No, no, no, man. Turn around."

All he wanted was a picture of himself with the back of my jacket.

This story always gets a nice response from the audience when I tell it. Well, not always. Once I told it and the audience just stared at me. They were confused. I was confused because they were confused. I had no idea why they didn't "get it," why they didn't laugh.

Later, my daughter, who was in the audience, solved the riddle. She said, "Dad, you never told them about the jacket." She was right. I had forgotten to mention that the USO gave us a jacket with a picture of Bob Hope on the back. Without that, the story made no sense.

I mention this because it's very easy for us, as writers, to *assume* that the readers know as much about what we're talking about as we do. Often they don't. As I was telling my jacket story, I could visualize that jacket as clearly as if I were wearing it at the time. I thought the audience could visualize it as well as I could. They not only couldn't visualize it; they had no idea that a jacket existed at all. It was my task to tell them about it during the story. It's the writer's obligation to tell the readers all that they need to know, also.

> As an example of assuming too much, I get frustrated when I try to do something different on my computer and I turn to the "help" button to find out how to do whatever it is I'm trying to do. Let's say I'm trying to do something fancy with the fonts. The instructions I get when I call up "help" tell me to "select Option B in the Font Options Panel." However, they don't tell me how to get to the Font Options Panel. So I get out my instruction book, look in the index, and find no reference to a Font Options Panel. The writer apparently *assumes* we all know what a Font Options Panel is and how to get to it on the computer.

> As an author, I just completed a book about some of my television writing experiences. In there, I told a hilarious story about something that happened at our Wednesday run-through. The editor, of course, wrote in the margin, "I have no idea what a 'Wednesday run-through' is." Naturally, I had to edit the text and explain what a run-through was. (It is a rehearsal that we typically held on Wednesday afternoon in which the cast performed the entire show from start to finish—hence the phrase "run-through.")

The same thing can happen in fiction writing, when the author knows something about the characters that is important to the plot, but neglects to tell the readers. It can happen easily.

So, in keeping with the first admonition here to "TAKE YOUR TIME," explain any concepts that your readership might not know. Don't assume that your readers know as much about your topic or your characters as you do. Of course, you don't want to write as if you're writing for kindergartners, but it is safer to be more informative than you have to be rather than to omit important information.

ENTERTAIN YOUR READERS

You write a book so that people will read it. People will read it if it's fun to read. Certainly, as an author, you must convey ideas. In a nonfiction book, you're offering information. In a fiction book, you're offering a story. In both cases, though, the offering will be more effective (and more accepted) if it's an "entertaining read."

There is a certain *showmanship* to writing. Add a little pizzazz to whatever information you're supplying. As I mentioned in talking about comedians, you not only offer your readers fun, but you have fun along with them. And you invite them to have fun along with you. By "fun," in this case, I don't mean guffaws or belly laughs. But I do mean that your book should be enjoyable for folks to read.

So, with these thoughts in mind, I recommend that you write one of your chapters now. It will give you an idea of how beneficial planning your book and allowing your chapter to "marinate" can be. It will also give you a feel for how your writing will progress. You'll know how much effort you have to expend to write a chapter. You'll get an inkling for how long it will take you to generate a chapter. Also, if you incorporate all of the above suggestions into your writing of a chapter, you'll begin to get a feel for how long each chapter will be.

CHAPTER 9

HOW BIG A BOOK DO YOU PLAN TO WRITE?

Some writing definitely has size constraints. When I wrote my first screenplay and turned it over to my agent, he called and told me the writing was fine, but the script was sixty pages too long. I had to cut the screenplay by 30 percent before he would submit it to production companies.

For almost ten years, I wrote a monthly humor column for a magazine. The editor asked that I keep each article within 800 to 850 words. They wanted each piece to fit on one page of the magazine. Later, they added larger illustrations and asked me to reduce the size of each submission to a maximum of 750 words. Those articles I had already written and submitted had to be cut back to accommodate the new page layout.

Television sitcoms are restricted by time. Any script you write must fit into the thirty minute television time slot (allowing time for commercials and promos and such). Anything more or anything less is unacceptable.

A book, though, can be any length. It can be as short as *Jonathan Livingston Seagull* or as overwhelmingly long as *War and Peace.* Nevertheless, it's wise to have a pretty good idea of how large your intended manuscript will be. Why? Well, because this is the phase of the program when you're about to develop your writing schedule. You remember—the one you're going to adhere to religiously. In order to figure out how much time you're going to allow for your writing, you should know approximately how much writing you're going to have to do. In other words, how big a book do you plan to write?

The previous chapter advised you to write at least one chapter of your book. This exercise served several purposes. First, if you review Chapter 1 (So What's Keeping You from Writing Your Book?) of this book, you'll see that the number-one reason listed for books not being completed was that they were never begun. It seems obvious that you cannot complete a book if you never start writing the book. So, congratulations! With the completion of that chapter, you've now officially started writing your book. That's not only a commendable first step; it's a mandatory first step.

Second, writing your initial chapter gives you a feeling for how much of a chore it will be for you to write the remaining chapters of your book. Of course, each segment of the book you write will have its own particular pitfalls, problems, and delays. Some chapters may be easy for you to write; others will be more challenging. But this first one provides at least a clue as to how much effort the remainder of the writing will require.

The third benefit of having already written one chapter is that you should now have an idea about what amount of time you'll have to devote to each chapter. If you paid attention to the notes you made and allowed time for the chapter to marinate, you went through the entire process of planning and writing a chapter. That's a fair indicator of how long it should take you to write a typical chapter.

Fourth, writing the chapter allows you to measure how large your subsequent chapters will be. Again, of course, the individual chapters will vary in length, and there's no necessity to limit the word count of each section of your book. Nevertheless, you should have an average word count to shoot for. As I mentioned earlier, my humor columns were limited to approximately 800 to 850 words. I couldn't average those out by writing an article one month that was 400 words long and then one for the following month that was 1200 words long. *Each* article had to fill a magazine page that could accommodate 800 to 850 words. With your book, though, you can average out—and, in fact, you should average out—the chapter lengths. Writing each chapter to the exact word count of the one before it would not only become monotonous, it would impose an artificial constraint that would stretch some chapters too thin and force important information to be left out of others. It would make for tedious reading and very restrictive writing. If for no other reason than variety, some chapters should be long and others short. Nevertheless, it will be beneficial if you have a good average word count to shoot for. For example, if you have thirty chapters and you are planning a book of approximately 60,000 words, you must average 2,000 words per chapter.

Referring to Chapter 1 again, you'll recall that the third reason listed for not completing a book is that you didn't have a book in the first place. By writing this initial chapter of your book, you have an idea of how long your chapters will be (on average) and you know from your completed outline how many chapters you have. Now you can multiply the two to determine how large a book you intend to write and, of course, if that is enough to fill a reasonably sized book.

For instance, suppose you discover that the chapter you wrote was 800 words long and you have twelve chapters listed in your book outline. That will generate a manuscript of only 9,600 words. In most cases, that's hardly enough to fill a book. The quote I mentioned earlier from one of my writing colleagues would apply in this case: "I started out to write a book and wound up with a pamphlet."

As an example, I've taken the planning I've done on this book you're presently reading and averaged out the word count of those chapters I've written so far. They average approximately 3000 words. I presently envision 20 chapters in the book. So the total word count will come to about 60,000 words, appropriate for a book of this type.

> I've maintained that even with exhaustive planning, your book can remain flexible until it's printed and sent out to bookstores. The example I've used concerning this volume is a fitting illustration of that.
>
> After the manuscript was written, the publisher and I decided to eliminate several chapters in order to keep the material more concise and pertinent. Rather than the 20 chapters I mentioned above, we reduced it to 16 chapters.
>
> This reduced the word count to 45,000 words, which we both felt was enough for this type of book.

If you do your own quick calculations, though, and discover that your text is a tad thin, there are remedies available to you. First, you can try to get more substance into each chapter, boosting the word count. How do you add more substance? Your salient points may be bolstered with amusing anecdotes or even jokes that are apropos. You may give examples of people who successfully used the techniques you're recommending. Often, I will offer advice and then support it with the benefits that will result from following that advice. And, of course, you can always offer quotes from famous people that validate your opinions.

As an example, in one of my books I was making the point that humor is an effective device for communicating. To add substance to this idea, I cited many humorous quotes from Abraham Lincoln—a decisive leader, a consummate communicator, and of course, a great president. Then I told how Lincoln was criticized for his jokes. It was considered unbecoming "buffoonery" by many of his political associates. Lincoln explained that he didn't tell his tales to amuse the listeners or to draw applause from them, but rather because his stories reduced complex issues to simple anecdotes that could be readily understood by all the people. This not only added several amusing stories to the text, but it also made the point that an effective leader was using humor to educate and communicate.

Second, you may try to come up with additional chapters, filling out your book a bit more.

Third, you can determine that your book is special and it is worth writing regardless of the size or number of the chapters and the total word count. *The Elements of Style*, written by William Strunk, Jr. and E. B. White, is a tiny volume, yet it remains a classic, best-selling guide for writers almost 100 years after it was first published.

Any one of those solutions is acceptable, because this is your book and you can write it the way you want to write it.

In any case, you know how many chapters you have in your outline. You know approximately how many words will be in each chapter. And you have a good idea of how long it will take you to plan and write each chapter. With that information, you're now ready to prepare the writing schedule for the book you've always wanted to write.

CHAPTER 10

PLAN YOUR WRITING SCHEDULE

An organized, well-thought-out writing schedule is the heart of this system for starting and writing that book you've always wanted to write. It keeps the project alive. It incorporates all of the elements we spoke of earlier that are necessary for writing a book.

■ **Focus:** Being obliged to complete a certain number of pages or chapters each day or week keeps you focused on having to get some work done on your book. It doesn't permit you to forget that you are working on a project.

  With specific tasks to complete at specific times, the schedule keeps you focused on writing a specific part of your book. Remember, that was the stipulation you accepted as part of my writing system—that you would write only a part of your book at any given time.

■ **Organization:** By definition, you must be organized to create an organized schedule. Once created, the schedule keeps your writing systematic. You're no longer writing randomly. Your writing in a structured fashion towards a pre-set goal. You're work plan is arranged efficiently enough for you to keep records so you can know how well you've progressed and how much you still have to accomplish.

■ **Momentum:** In order to complete the specified writing assignments in the allotted time, you must keep writing on a regular basis. The schedule precludes stop-and-start writing. Once you begin this writing, following a well-conceived plan, you continue working at a reasonable pace until the project is finished. And that is the ultimate goal of this plan.

■ **Discipline:** The schedule demands that you plan your project and that you write according to that plan. It doesn't permit you to wait until the muse visits you. It doesn't afford you the luxury of writing only when *you feel like writing.* It dictates that you write when the schedule says you write. That requires willpower and a serious commitment. And it will result in you arriving at your sought-after destination: a finished manuscript.

WHAT GOES INTO A WELL-CONCEIVED WRITING SCHEDULE

Before you formulate your writing schedule, let's consider some of the characteristics of a workable plan. To be effective, your schedule should be:

- Detailed
- Realistic
- Challenging
- Reasonable
- Generous.

Let's analyze each of these characteristics.

■ **Detailed:** Your schedule should have firm dates, a set amount of work to be completed in a given amount of time, and it should be measurable. For example, if your plan says that by October 30th (a definite date) you will have completed four chapters (a set amount of work), that's a definite goal. If you have completed four chapters by the end of October, that's a measurable accomplishment. If you haven't completed those chapters, you're not adhering to your schedule. You have some catching up to do or some adjustments to make to your writing plan.

For the purposes of this plan, vague schedules are virtually worthless. For instance, "I'll have part of a chapter written by the end of the month." Another example would be, "I plan to finish this book within a year." These types of promises are too easy to postpone. You can remember from your school days that when you put off your homework or your studies until they *had* to be done, you usually found on the day before they were due that they weren't done. Not only were they not completed, but there was not enough time to complete them. That's what can happen with vague scheduling.

I recommend that you keep the planning segments short, one week at a time. You may feel there is no difference between "I'll write four chapters a month" and "I'll write one chapter each week." But there is a difference. If your goal is write one chapter a week, and at the end of the week you haven't done that, you're behind schedule. You may have to work harder, faster, or sacrifice some of your free time to get back on track. On the other hand, if you plan to write four chapters a month, and at the end of the first week you haven't written anything, you're not behind schedule. You're not behind until the end of the fourth week, but by then you might be too far behind to catch up. It may be a subtle difference, but it has major consequences on your prospects for success.

If you want to complete a chapter by the end of the month, decide which portion of that chapter you'll complete in the first week. Then plan how much you'll finish by the end of the second week, and so on. That way, you can measure your progress weekly and be more likely to complete a chapter by the end of the month.

If you promise that you'll write your book within a year, determine what amount of work you'll do in each week of that year. As the weeks pass, you can measure your progress and calibrate your writing so that at the end of that year you'll have a completed manuscript in hand.

When you finance the purchase of a car, you'll find that the company furnishing the money will also furnish a payment schedule. They'll require a certain amount of cash to be paid each month. You'll have a hard time finding a company that will allow you a vague repayment schedule. No lending company is going to forward you $25,000 dollars and say, "Just pay it back to us after four years." Instead, they'll provide a payment plan that is clearly spelled out and measurable.

That's what you should want from your writing schedule.

■ **Realistic:** You have a wonderful idea for a book right now. The world deserves to read what you're going to write. However, the world is going to have to wait. The concept you have needs development, it needs planning, it requires execution. All of these things take time. Be sure in planning your schedule that you allow enough time to give your book the devotion it requires. Be realistic about how much time it will take you to deliver a well-planned, well-executed manuscript.

For example, suppose you've got a publisher interested in a book you've proposed, a book that you absolutely know will take you exactly four months to write. (I'm not sure how you would know that, but let's just assume you do know it.) Can you then promise that publisher that you will deliver the first draft of the manuscript in four months? Most likely not.

Why? Well, it should take you a certain amount of time to plan and organize your book. And, even if you can complete the text within the four months, you'll still need time to prepare it for submission. You'll want to reread your work, make corrections, do some rewriting, get those revisions into the copy, perhaps repaginate, run off hard copies, make a file to present to the publisher, and maybe do a few more things that you haven't yet considered.

Be realistic and realize that writing the manuscript is only part of the entire process.

Also, you must be realistic and admit that writing this book is not your entire life. You can't schedule it as if it were. You may have a day job that requires a great deal of your time, quite possibly eight hours a day or more. You have family matters that demand your time and attention. Unforeseen emergencies could interfere. These things must be considered in planning an effective writing schedule. In other words, remember that you're scheduling your writing time, not your entire, unpredictable life.

Being realistic requires that you admit that you're human. Sure, you have a book you want to write now. You're enthused about that book. You feel almost superhuman in the amount of writing you can do. However, I've repeated a few times that writing a book is not an effortless task. I use the terms "writing your book" and "working on your book" interchangeably because writing becomes work. One writing colleague of mine used to say, "When did my career suddenly become a job?" It's true. Working on a book, though fun, can become physically and mentally demanding.

As a gag writer, I could write about thirty jokes an hour. That doesn't mean that in an 8-hour workday I could turn out 240 gags. It certainly doesn't mean that if I put in a 12-hour workday I could turn out 360 funny items. Why doesn't the math hold up? If I can write thirty jokes an hour, why isn't it true that I could write eight times that amount in eight hours? It's because weariness sets in. After writing a certain amount of gags, I tire of that process. Maybe I can continue to type, but I don't continue to write as well.

Consider a track star who can sprint the 100-yard dash in ten seconds. That's a good time. Using pure math, that same person should be able to complete a mile run in about 2.9 minutes. That's an incredible time. In fact, it's an impossible time. That would require the runner to run at full speed for the entire mile. It can't be done.

No, the fatigue factor enters into the equation and the runner has to adjust the pace for the longer distance. Writers, too, have to pace themselves for the long distance. That's only being realistic.

■ **Challenging:** Earlier, we noted that vague schedules are practically useless. When one says, "I'll finish this book within a year," that effectively leaves fifty-one weeks out of that year with no real challenge confronting you. You don't have to finish anything the first week because you've still got fifty-one other weeks to catch up. You don't have any required production for the second week either because fifty weeks is plenty of time to recover. And, if you continue on in this way, you'll find yourself eight or nine months into your schedule with little writing done, plagued by a growing sense of anxiety.

By the same token, a schedule that doesn't demand application can be just as useless. For example, suppose you create a schedule that requires you to write one chapter every six months. It's fairly obvious that you'll abandon that routine quickly. Any writing schedule that's too easy can cause you to lose interest, which could result in forgetting about the project all together.

In order to continue the momentum of writing your book, you must remain enthused about the project. A challenging schedule keeps you excited about your writing.

■ **Reasonable:** However, you don't want your writing plan to be too challenging. You don't want it to be impossible: "I'll write ten chapters a week. That way, in three weeks, I'll have my book finished." No, you won't. You'll have a splitting headache, a heart full of disappointment, and a resolve that you'll never be able to write a worthwhile book. Putting too heavy a demand upon yourself is probably more counterproductive than creating too easy a schedule. At least an easy schedule is do-able. An impossible schedule is not.

The burden is on you to balance a challenging schedule and an overly challenging plan. Here, you must be honest with yourself. You must decide how much you can reasonably accomplish in a given period of time. You might push yourself a little bit beyond your comfort zone, but be careful not to force yourself beyond your limits.

As you get into the actual planning of your schedule, I'll suggest that you allow time for rest or to reward yourself for exceptional work. I'll also recommend that you include some adjustments within your schedule so that you can fine-tune this balance between a challenging routine and an impossible routine.

- **Generous:** In planning a complete schedule, be generous to yourself. Give yourself the benefit of the doubt. Let's go back to that hypothetical that we discussed earlier: a publisher is interested in a book that you proposed, a book that you "knew" you could write in four months. Assuming all of that is still applicable, what sort of schedule would you devise so that you could furnish the publisher with a firm date for delivery? For the reasons we noted earlier, you certainly wouldn't promise it for four months from now.

  You would probably crank in a certain amount of time for proper planning of the entire writing project. You'd still allow the four months (or maybe a bit more) for the writing of the text. Then you'd give yourself time to reread, rewrite, retype, and prepare your total package for delivery to the publisher.

  Being "generous to yourself" means that you allow time for unforeseen problems in this process. Why? Because publishers don't mind getting a manuscript early. It gives them time to do whatever planning is required by their staff to get the book into print. However, they dislike authors who fail to meet deadlines. This puts them off schedule and may cost them extra money in order to meet their publishing dates. So rather than cut the dates too close, you're better off giving yourself a little bit of extra time.

  This obtains, also, if you're working to a deadline that you've created yourself. You'll feel much better about your entire project if you're working to a schedule that you can comfortably meet. If you put yourself too far behind, you're creating stress that you don't need. You're forcing yourself into an uncomfortable position that could affect your writing. You're also taking a bit of fun out of the entire process. Remember, you want to maintain the momentum of your writing and also keep your enthusiasm in play. So allow yourself a reasonably generous grace period in your scheduling.

TASKS TO BE CONSIDERED IN ORGANIZING YOUR SCHEDULE

There are three areas you must consider in formulating any writing schedule: Planning, Writing the Text, and Preparing the Text for Publication.

■ **Planning** is a vital part of completing a book. Consider this book you're reading. We're up to Chapter 10 and you've only written one chapter of your book. Most of this text has been devoted to planning and preparation. It's tempting to think that the sooner you start writing your manuscript, the sooner you'll complete it. That's not necessarily true. In fact, in most cases, it's false. Writing a book is a major endeavor, and beginning to write one without proper planning and thorough preparation can often lead to confusion during the writing process, which can delay or even derail the entire project. It can result in a considerable amount of unnecessary rewriting, which again delays the completion of the book.

Another concept to remember is that *momentum* is an important part of this program. Once you begin writing, the ideal is to continue writing at a reasonably consistent rate. It's easier to do that if you have a well-mapped-out plan in place.

So it's wise to allow generous time in your writing schedule for planning and preparation.

■ **Writing the Text** is obviously an inescapable task in completing a book. No book ever gets written without being written. It should be the major part of your writing schedule.

■ **Preparing the Text for Publication**, though, is also required. Once you've written your manuscript, you'll want to reread it. As you reread, you'll spot typos, flawed sentence structure, words you don't particularly like. You'll notice many things you'll want to change, improve, or delete, and so you'll change, improve, or delete them. However, that takes time. The entire manuscript must be revised and probably reprinted before you can submit it to the publisher. Allow time for that in your schedule.

CREATING YOUR SCHEDULE

Now let's get to the creation of your schedule.

The ultimate purpose of your writing schedule is to get your project completed by a specific date. However, there are two types of dates you may have to meet. The first is a hard date that has been determined by the contract for your book. If you're fortunate enough to have a contract in hand, it will surely have a delivery date spelled out. Once you sign and return that contract, you're obligated to meet that deadline.

So, let's just say, for the purposes of illustration, that you signed your contract on January 1st and have agreed to provide a completed first draft to the publisher on June 30th. That gives you six months to complete a publishable manuscript. However, as we've already discussed, you can't devote the entire six months to writing the text. You should give yourself a sufficient amount of time to prepare before writing and you should allow a generous amount of time after you've completed your writing to get the text ready to submit. The part in between is all you have left to write your book.

January 1st to June 30th gives you approximately twenty-four weeks of scheduling time. Let's assume you assign six weeks to preparing to write and another four weeks to preparing the finished text for submission. That leaves fourteen weeks to actually write the text.

With a hard deadline, you *must* complete your text in that amount of time. Also, in that time frame, you must plan for rest time, rewards to yourself, unforeseen events, and such. So, let's consider a possible schedule. Again, just for the purposes of illustration, let's assume you have twenty chapters in this book.

WEEK	CHAPTER	# OF WORDS	CHAPTER	# OF WORDS
#1	Yes - 1		Yes - 2	
#2	Yes - 3		Yes - 4	
#3	Yes - 5		Yes - 6	
Week #4.....................rest or rewriting				
#5	Yes - 7		Yes - 8	
#6	Yes - 9		Yes - 10	
#7	Yes - 11		No	
Week #8.....................rest or rewriting				
#9	Yes - 12		Yes - 13	
#10	Yes - 14		Yes - 15	
#11	Yes - 16		No	
Week #12.....................rest or rewriting				
#13	Yes - 17		Yes -18	
#14	Yes - 19		Yes - 20	

(NOTE: The numbers in the above schedule are not necessarily representative of the actual chapter numbers. As we discussed, you are free to write the chapters out of sequence. These numbers represent the *amount of chapters* you have completed within that given time frame.)

This, of course, is simply a sample schedule. In some weeks it demands completing two full chapters. During other weeks it allows you to write only one chapter, providing a chance to catch up should you fall a bit behind. There are weeks with no text writing scheduled. This can be either "vacation" time, another opportunity to catch up, or an opportunity to do some reviewing and rewriting.

The scheduling of your own writing, naturally, is up to you. You have an idea, from the chapter you've already written, how long it will take you to complete most chapters. You should know if you can conveniently produce two chapters a week or not. Maybe you can produce three. It's your project to maneuver.

Suppose, though, you don't have a contracted deadline or a predetermined date for the delivery of your manuscript. Then you have the option of manufacturing a deadline. You can set a reasonable completion date just for the sake of giving yourself a demanding challenge that will inspire you to get your book written. You, in essence, create *a contract with yourself*. If you do that, then you plan out your book exactly as we did above.

Another option, though, is to figure out how much you have to do, estimate how much time it will take you to do it, and set up your writing schedule, which will establish your completion date. For instance, you determine that you are able to write two chapters each week. You have twenty-six chapters, therefore you should allow thirteen weeks of actual writing time in your plan. You estimate sufficient planning time, maybe give yourself a few weeks off from your writing, add in certain weeks for preparing the manuscript for publication, and that calculation will generate your completion date.

A reminder, though, if you do select this option: Keep the schedule challenging. It must be demanding enough to maintain your interest in the project and allow you to keep your writing momentum.

Regardless of how you plan your schedule, there is the possibility that you could fall behind. What then? Well, you can use some of the free time that you've cranked into the writing plan to try to get back on schedule. That's one of the purposes of leaving a bit of free space available; it allows you to readjust your schedule. For instance, in the above sample schedule, we had some weeks where you planned to write one chapter only, instead of two.

Now that you're behind, you may have to alter that and produce two chapters in those weeks in order to catch up.

It may be, though, that regardless of how much time you put into your writing, you can't keep up with the schedule you've designed. Then you must give in to reality and redesign your plan. Move your completion date back and re-organize, working to a new schedule that is more reasonable, more in tune with your writing pace. If you're working to a self-imposed deadline that you manufactured, that's fine. You can change that date at will. But if you're working to a contracted deadline, it would be wise to warn the publisher, well in advance, that you may be late and negotiate a different deadline.

Be careful if you're allowing your work pace to determine the completion date. Pushing it back too often or too far might give you the excuse to keep postponing the work you're doing, and you run the danger of postponing your book right out of completion. Remember in Chapter I (So What's Keeping You From Writing Your Book?) how I noted one of the reasons for not completing a book was that "You Start Your Book, but Keep Postponing It Until You Finally Abandon It."

Of course, there's also the delightful possibility that you could get ahead of your schedule. What then? You could just continue on. Being ahead of schedule is not a problem. No publisher will ever be upset with an author who turns in a completed manuscript early. And, you, of course, won't be upset if you finish your book ahead of when you planned to finish it. If you have the energy and the resolve, keep on writing.

Or you could take a vacation. Remember, we said that the schedule should have some rest time included. This could be it. You've worked hard. You've earned a break. Take it and enjoy it.

Also, if you're ahead of schedule, you could use this time to work on items related to your project. For instance, you may create some sidebars that could be included in your book. These are items related to your main text, but they are not included as part of that text. An example might be if you tell a story about a famous person, you could include a sidebar that gives further information about that person—what school she attended, when, what sports records she holds, what she is doing currently, and so on. Sidebars can add information to your text without interfering with the flow of your writing. They can also add more substance to your book.

You could think of people that you might invite to write endorsements for your book or even supply a foreword or an introduction. You could write the back cover or inside flap text for your book. Someone has to do it. Why not you, now that you've got the time? Or, you might write "About the Author" information to be included in your book.

This available time could be used to think of marketing ideas for your book.

Why not make a list of people who are going to get free copies of your book? Once it's published, you're going to want to get copies into the hands of your friends. If you make a list now, there's less chance that you'll forget someone later.

You might also use this time to review what you've already written. Reread those chapters you've completed. Note typos or revisions and accordingly update your computer files. It could save you time when you get ready to prepare your text for publication.

One caution, though—if you get too far ahead, it can be unwise to apply too much of that time to "vacation." You do want to maintain the momentum and the enthusiasm for your project. If you take too much time away from it, you may find it hard to return to the task.

MAKE YOUR SCHEDULE "RESULTS ORIENTED"

Before leaving this chapter on planning your writing schedule, let's consider another form of scheduling: regularly devoting a definite amount of hours to writing. As an example, "From Monday to Friday, I'll work exclusively on my book from 8 A.M. until noon." That certainly exhibits discipline. If you stick to it, it may create momentum.

However, I don't recommend this type of scheduling because there is a subtle danger to this approach that can sabotage your chances of completing the book you've always wanted to write. What is this danger? Simply put, there's no guarantee that merely putting in man-hours will produce results. It's better, after a certain amount of work, to be able to show a definite end result rather than simply a vague satisfaction that "I've worked four hours on my book." All of us, with our busy schedules, must of course set aside time to work on our writing. I have no quarrel with that. In fact, that sort of discipline is commendable. However—and it's a big however—the time you set aside for working on your project should be accompanied by a definite, measurable goal.

A schedule that demands only "time put in" doesn't promote two important elements of this program. First, it lacks focus. Sure, you've dedicated a certain amount of hours to working on your project, but working on what? Are you allowing a chapter to marinate? Are you doing research? Are you actually typing text? Which chapter are you writing? Actually, after spending four hours working on your project, it may turn out that all you have to show for it is four hours of working on your project.

Second, it lacks organization. There's no real function to this scheduling system except to sit at your keyboard or your desk and do *something*. What provides solid organization is when you define that *something*. Isn't it more productive to say, "I'll work from 8 A.M. this Monday morning until noon, thinking about and making substantial notes on Chapter 1 of my book? On Tuesday, I'll take those notes and work for four hours on writing the text. If possible, I'll finish that chapter by noon on Tuesday. If not, I'll spend my four hours of work on Wednesday completing that chapter. I will have Chapter 1 completed by Wednesday."

So the discipline of setting regular working hours is commendable, but this program recommends that your schedule should be results-oriented. Develop the system of getting something done, as opposed to simply *putting in the hours*.

Earlier, I said this scheduling system of devoting so many hours to your work *may create momentum*. However, it might also destroy your momentum if it's not coupled with a goal-oriented schedule. Even if you're faithful to dedicating so many hours a day to your writing project, that doesn't lead you to completing your book unless you're achieving some measurable progress towards that goal. It can become a valid excuse for abandoning the project altogether. Who can fault you for quitting if you can honestly say, "I've been working my tail off on this book and I'm getting nowhere"?

So, my program's recommendation is that you set up goals to meet along the way. Figure out a reasonable amount of time to meet those goals. Make that the heart of your schedule and then measure your progress as you go and comfortably work your way towards the completion of your book.

CHAPTER 11

GET YOUR BOOK TO THE MARKET PLACE

You've reached a point in this program where you're beginning to write your book, chapter by chapter. Depending on the schedule you've devised, you now have three, four, five, or more months to complete your manuscript. However, in planning your book and preparing to write, you've also done much work that can be used to market your book. You began this program by describing your book to yourself. That description can be refined and made part of your query letter.

You know which chapters you'll include in your manuscript and you've written a synopsis of each one.

You've researched and written about other books already in the marketplace and how the one you're writing offers something different. You've addressed why you are the person to write your book. You know who your potential readers are. All of these can become a part of your book proposal.

You worked on these aspects of your book in order to help you get your project started and to continue onward until completion. All of these documents can also be used to market your book *while you're busy writing it*.

There are two major instruments that you can use to begin marketing your book: the query letter and the book proposal. You can begin circulating one or both of these documents to agents and publishers. In the Introduction of this book (What This Book Is and Is Not), I stated clearly that this would not be an instructional book on writing style or technique. Nor is it a treatise on marketing your book. It's simply a program that guides you in starting and finishing the book you've always wanted to write. Therefore, in these pages, I won't go into the details of composing a query letter or a book proposal. There are well-written, informative books already on the shelves that do this. Check the Internet booksellers or your neighborhood bookstores to find worthwhile volumes on these subjects.

Nevertheless, having a contract in hand or agents or publishers who show interest in your book can be an incentive to complete your manuscript. So, let's discuss some tips on submitting your volume for consideration as you're busy completing it.

Actually, this is not an integral part of this program for starting and completing your book. You're free to decide whether to submit your book now or wait until you have a completed manuscript. There are some benefits to circulating your book at this point, but there are also some caveats. We'll discuss these briefly and then you can decide.

POSSIBLE BENEFITS

1. **Eliminates Dead Time:** "Dead time" is that period where you are waiting for a response. You write to an agent or a publisher and you're eager to receive a reply. This waiting time can be stressful and it can be painful. It can also inhibit productivity. Many writers send out a submission letter and then do nothing else creatively until they receive feedback. By sending your submission letters out now, you can't afford to do nothing as you wait for a reply. You still have a book to write and a definite schedule to adhere to. Consequently, you're utilizing that dead time. Not only that, but you're distracting yourself from the anguish of anticipating a "yea" or a "nay" from publishers or agents. You're much too busy writing to fret about what they have to say.

2. **Periodic Responses Keep the Book Alive:** Remember that part of this program is to keep your writing momentum and your enthusiasm in play. One of the ideas we spoke of earlier that can keep a book from getting written is that you postpone activity on it so often that you eventually abandon the project. You simply forget about it. Receiving responses to your submissions every so often does, at the very least, remind you that you are busy with a project. Certainly, a positive response will lift your enthusiasm. That's good. It prompts you to return to your task with renewed vigor. However, even negative feedback reminds you that you're still working on this project.

3. **There's Always the Possibility of a Sale:** Submitting your book now is not a guarantee that an agent or a publisher will send you a contract. However, not submitting your book is a guarantee that neither an agent nor a publisher will send a contract. In other words, if you do,

you have a chance; if you don't, you have no chance. If you want to sell this book, you're going to have to go through the submission ritual sometime. Submitting your project now just might generate interest, and that's a fantastic incentive to complete the manuscript.

POTENTIAL DISADVANTAGES

1. **This Process Could Be Distracting:** Your main goal is to finish a book. Query letters and book proposals, even though you've done much of the work already as part of preparing to write, still require time and effort. They are your introductions to the marketplace. You want them to be professional, effective, and representative of your work as a writer. They should be as polished (some say even more polished) than your final product. In order to get them to that level, you have to give them all of your expertise. You may decide that your devotion should be directed toward your project instead. You might determine that your energies should all flow in one direction at a time. Do the book; then do the marketing. The choice is yours, and either decision is valid.

2. **You Will Get Rejections:** Rejection is part of the writer's life. All authors at all levels face rejection. Regardless of sales record or success, each writer gets rejected in some way at some time or another. The publisher may object to a certain ending. The editor may recommend dropping an entire chapter. The agent may ask for numerous changes before beginning to submit your book. Of course, successful authors with proven sales potential may be able to ignore some of these rejections. Nevertheless, they remain "rejections." If you submit your idea now, you will surely get some negative response. That's a given. The question, however, is how you will respond to the negativity. One, two, or three rejection form letters in a week could demoralize you. It could derail your momentum and your enthusiasm. This is a risk you may opt to avoid. If you don't send out submissions, you can be absolutely certain that you won't get rejection letters. You might decide that's the safer way to proceed until you at least get your book written.

A NOTE ABOUT REJECTION

Since rejection is such an integral part of writing, at all stages, let's discuss it briefly before moving on to writing your text.

First, as a writer you must recognize that rejections are inevitable. That's not a negative statement nor is it meant to discourage passionate writers. It's simply a statement of fact. Learning to deal with rejection realistically can help you maintain your exuberance for your writing. Be prepared to accept negative replies. One salesman told me that he *relished* rejection. His reasoning was that he recognized that only ten percent of the clients he called on would buy from him. Therefore, he had to wade through nine refusals before he got one sale. So the quicker he got the nine out of the way, the sooner he got to the one buyer.

When I began my joke writing career, I would visit with any comedian who came to my town. I would show them my gags and hope to sell a few or even land a contract. Many of the comics looked at my material and said "no." A few of them looked and said worse things than "no." Then I showed my gags to Phyllis Diller. She bought some. She bought more. She began to buy regularly. She offered me a contract. She offered me a staff writing job on her television show. This was the start of a long career.

Did I continue to fret about the comedians who refused my material? No. I simply delighted in the fact that one comic liked my stuff. That was enough to build a career.

Second, consider that rejection is not always a bad thing. Granted, it's usually painful when you experience it, but often it can produce beneficial results. I worked in a large manufacturing plant before I began my writing career. There we'd periodically have *head-rolling sessions*. That's rather a grim, cruel term for "layoffs." Certain people would be pink-slipped, let go, fired—whatever you call it, it meant they were being terminated.

That always seemed disastrous to them at the time. The common thinking was that they were out of work as of Friday afternoon, and they would be out of work forever. It never developed that way. People found new jobs and, in fact, some advanced into more creative and eventually higher-paying jobs. The possibility is that they would never have found that success in their new jobs if they hadn't been fired from their old jobs.

So there's always a chance that a rejection could result in a blessing. Will it always? Maybe not, but it's rarely as catastrophic as we tend to imagine it.

Third, realize that negative responses are neither condemnations nor criticism of your work. All a rejection says is that this buyer is not prepared at this time to buy your wares. That doesn't imply that your work is not salable. It simply means it's not going to sell at this time to this buyer.

Let me offer another example from show business. As the producer of a television sitcom, I once had to hire an actress for one episode. Our show needed only one actress, but I contacted several agents and auditioned twenty young ladies for the role. The math is obvious: One girl would get the job and nineteen would be turned down.

After all of the girls read for the part, our creative staff had several discussions about which actress to hire. Some liked Mary; others preferred Charlotte. A few wanted to hire Charlene; others thought Mildred was much more talented. Eventually, we settled on one, but we were astounded by the talent that most of those girls displayed. Yes, nineteen of them didn't get the job, but that didn't mean those nineteen couldn't act.

In fact, an addendum to this story reinforces what we spoke of earlier—rejections can turn into blessings. The following year, I was producing a different sitcom and had to hire a girl to be a regular. I hired one of the nineteen that I didn't hire for the single episode. Being turned down for a one-time role resulted in the young lady being hired for an entire season.

Here are just a few reasons why a manuscript might be rejected:

1. The publisher's schedule is full.
2. There's no budget for new product at this time.
3. The publisher has a similar book already in the works.
4. Your book may compete with the works of some of the publisher's established authors.
5. The publishers don't want to reduce the sales potential of those authors.
6. The publishers don't want to make those authors unhappy.
7. It may just be the wrong type of subject for this particular publisher.
8. The publisher may not agree with your concept.
9. The publisher may feel your book doesn't have enough sales potential.
10. The publisher may feel your book does have sales potential but that their company is not equipped to handle this particular book properly.
11. The publisher may just hate the book. But publishers can be wrong!

So, you can opt to submit your book at this point or delay the marketing until you've completed your work on it. Once you've made your decision, though, it's time to move on to the writing of the text, chapter by chapter. Let's do it.

CHAPTER 12

WRITING YOUR BOOK CHAPTER BY CHAPTER

THIS PHASE OF THE PROGRAM—writing the text for your book—is entirely in your hands. I've stated repeatedly that this is not a book of writing instruction. The technique and the style are totally up to you. This program doesn't involve itself with spelling, punctuation, or sentence structure—those are all your concern. In fact, this process doesn't even care if you decide to use a preposition to end a sentence with. This is your book; you write it.

That said, though, I will offer the following tips on the procedure of writing that will help you to persevere in this project until it is completed—since "completion" is the ultimate goal of this system:

LET EACH CHAPTER MARINATE

"Marinate" is a term I use for thinking through each chapter before you take it to the keyboard. The thinking can be almost subliminal, where you continue on with your other activities but allow the chapter to remain in your head, doing whatever it does in there. You should allow some time for active concentration, too. Spend some time pondering what you'll cover in the chapter you're about to write. Do whatever research you need to do. Gather anecdotes, examples, and illustrations. Lay out the flow of the chapter—how you'll open, which ideas come next, and how you'll close. Plan out a few of the paragraphs you'll include in this chapter.

Most of this was discussed in Chapter 8 (WRITE A CHAPTER), so you might go back and reread that chapter as a review. However, I mention it again here to emphasize that this should be a regular practice in writing your manuscript.

Thinking each chapter through before writing it gives more depth to your book, and you increase the percentages of having considered and included all of the ideas that you want to get across to your readers.

By laying out the form of the entire chapter, your writing becomes more organized. One thought flows into the next in a logical sequence. Because your thinking and planning are more coordinated, the writing process becomes not only easier, but quicker. Planning helps you write more efficiently and more effectively.

A big factor in this program, as you well know by now, is *momentum*. Having a chapter planned out beforehand allows you to write practically without interruption. You don't start writing and then stop to do some needed research. You have it before you. If you want to emphasize a particular point, you needn't pause to consider an appropriate anecdote. You've already done that. Your examples, illustrations, and whatever fall into place as you write because you've already considered which ones to use and where to use them.

WRITE REGULARLY

Maintain a reasonably steady pace of writing. This doesn't mean that you should be mechanical about your writing. It's not necessary to show up at the keyboard at 8 A.M. each morning and work religiously until the lunch whistle sounds at noon. You don't have to chain yourself to the computer keyboard so that you put in a demanding number of hours.

No, what this tip suggests is that you show up at reasonable intervals to work on your project—that's all. Maybe you work every Monday, Wednesday, and Friday on your book. Perhaps, you're more comfortable working on Tuesdays and Thursdays. Maybe you show up at the keyboard only when you have a chapter set in your mind and you're ready to begin typing it.

The key idea here is that you don't permit too much time to go by between writing sessions once you begin the text. You want to maintain the *momentum*.

> Let me offer an example about momentum from my experience of writing for television variety shows. The writers on such shows would work on two levels: we'd be preparing material for upcoming shows, but we'd also be expected to write quick fixes and revisions to the current show. This was never a problem. If adjustments were quickly needed, we could all step aside from whatever future sketches we were working on and chip in with the necessary rewrite for this week's show. If we needed a new line immediately, the staff would produce it. If we

needed a funnier joke for this week's show, we'd turn it out quickly and add it to the script. Never a problem.

EXCEPT...near the end of the season. Why would this become a problem? The staff had no future shows to work on. They were all written. Consequently, we'd have to be available only if needed to adjust the current show. This left the staff with plenty of free time—non-writing time.

Then if the director or the producers would come to the writing staff for a new line or a funnier joke, we would have trouble supplying it. Why? Because our momentum had been destroyed. We got out of the habit of turning out material regularly. It would sometimes take an entire staff a complete day to turn out a line that we would have written in an hour during the height of the season.

That's how interrupting your writing for too long a period can affect your production and the quality of your product.

So, no, you don't have to be a meticulous taskmaster who demands a rigid hour-by-hour writing regimen. However, you should be getting to the keyboard and turning out text on a fairly regular basis.

FIND YOUR MOST PRODUCTIVE WRITING TIME

Each of us has a certain internal rhythm. Some of us are energetic in the morning. We rise and shine, and we sing and hum even before our first cup of coffee. Others don't look human until after noon. Bob Hope used to kid, "You're as young as you feel. And I don't feel anything until noon. By then it's time for my nap."

Throughout my television writing days, I liked to get to the desk early and start working. Morning was my most productive time. However, I've known writers who were only comfortable working on their scripts during the night, when most people were sleeping.

For whatever reasons, we have different productive cycles. It's wise for writers to discover those times when they work most effectively and utilize those times. Obviously, if you do, you'll get more done. You'll also get it done more quickly, more easily, and with more satisfying results.

You should have a pretty good feel for when you work best. For example, in my case, I just naturally get to the keyboard early in the day. I work there until about noon or a bit longer if I have a segment that I want to complete before taking a break. After lunch, if I have more work to do, I almost have to force myself back to the keyboard. The verve and the enthusiasm seems to disappear.

So investigate your own work habits and see if you can uncover your optimum working time. If you can't, you might experiment. In any case, when you're eager to work is when you should get most of your writing done.

If you're a morning person, write then. You can do other, more clerical work, during your "off-hours." For instance, your afternoon may be the time to attack some research you have to do or address and send out letters.

If you're an afternoon or an evening worker, then do the clerical stuff in the morning and save the writing for when you're more exuberant about it. In other words, do the creative work on your book when you are your most creative. Do your non-creative work during your non-creative hours.

AVOID BEING TOO JUDGMENTAL ABOUT YOUR WRITING

One time I took some monologue material to Bob Hope. He took the envelope from me, hefted it in his hands, and said, "I'm sure this stuff is brilliant." I wasn't really pleased with my output that day, so I said honestly, "Bob, I don't think it is." He seemed to be stunned that a writer would admit that his material wasn't hilarious, but he quickly recovered. He said to me, "Oh, well, that's OK. Some of the other writers will be brilliant."

That's pretty much the attitude that you should have about your writing as you're turning out the pages. Keep in mind that not all of it will be scintillating. Some will be ordinary. Let's be really honest—some of it will be terrible. But right now, as you're turning out pages, is not the time to be ultracritical.

Don't misunderstand, though. I didn't purposely turn out mediocre monologue jokes to hand to Bob Hope. I didn't intentionally slack off on my writing because I thought the other writers would cover for me. I worked hard on the assignment; I just didn't produce exemplary results this particular day.

There have been times when all of the writers turned out material that wasn't sparkling and we were asked to "run it through the typewriter again." In other words, do it over. Often, the rewrite or the new material would be brilliant. Mediocre material doesn't have to remain that way. Later, you'll have the opportunity to review your work, rewrite it, or even start some material from scratch. That's all part of this program.

At this phase, it's not wise to be too critical.

Again, this is not an invitation to write too quickly or lazily. Write each sentence and each paragraph as well as you know how. The danger of being too critical too soon is that it can destroy your enthusiasm. Writing a book is a difficult and time-consuming task. It doesn't get done in a day, a week, or a month. It requires considerable effort and time. Both of these are wearying. It's important to remain enthused in order to finish the project. Constantly being dissatisfied with your output can destroy that enthusiasm. It can prompt you to abandon the entire project. Obviously, that can't be good if your intent is to complete your book.

Here's another phenomenon you should be aware of—often your *medio-cre* material can turn brilliant all by itself. I know that sounds mysterious and abnormal, but it happens. Of course, the material doesn't rewrite itself. In fact, it doesn't change at all. What changes is your perception of it.

Sometimes we can be in a bad mood. Nothing we write pleases us. Because of our mood, we're dissatisfied with whatever pops up on our computer screen. To paraphrase a pretty good writer, William Shakespeare, "The fault lies not within our writing, but within ourselves." Often in this case, you'll persevere through your writing, reread it after whatever was bothering you has calmed down, and you'll discover that your words are not really as bad as you thought they were. It can happen.

Regardless, the important thing at this phase is to get your thoughts on paper without interfering with the process. Those words will stay on paper until you're ready to return to them. When you do reread them, you'll do it with pencil in hand, ready to revise, rewrite, or relegate to the waste basket and begin anew.

AVOID IMMEDIATE REWRITES

Get your words on paper and *leave them there for awhile.* They won't go anywhere. If you pop them into a loose-leaf book or slip them into a drawer, they'll stay there. They'll be the same when you take them out as they were when you put them in.

The words won't change, but you might. We just mentioned above that sometimes your attitude during your writing can taint your opinion of your work. Later, when your attitude has an adjustment, your writing may take on a new flavor, at least in your eyes. That's one reason to let the material sit for awhile.

Consider, too, that you have certain ideas running through your head as you type your material. These thoughts affect what you say and how you say it. They determine the words you put on paper. If you reread and rewrite your material as soon as it comes out of the printer, most of those thoughts and ideas in your head will still be there. They'll still influence your writing.

However, if you let the pages sit for a few days, even a week or so, by the time you return to them, you'll be seeing them with new eyes. You'll have a fresher view of your material. Your original thoughts will always be there because that's what you put on paper. Those are the ideas you typed. Now, however, you may have a few different thoughts. You may have a different perception of your original thinking. You may have additional ideas to add to what you've written.

If you rewrite too quickly, you may not be *rewriting* at all. You may simply be corroborating what you've already committed to paper. If you let your mind relax for awhile, you will probably return to the text better prepared to honestly analyze and evaluate it. You'll get better use of your rewriting time.

WRITE YOUR CHAPTERS IN ANY SEQUENCE

Remember, one of the benefits of preparing and planning your book so thoroughly was that it afforded you the luxury of writing out of sequence. With a comprehensive plan, you know what's going into your book, what material you're going to cover, and where it all fits into the overall project. This allows you to write any part of that plan at anytime with the assurance that it will conveniently fill the niche you've reserved for it in your manuscript.

This doesn't preclude you from starting with Chapter 1 and continuing until you get to the back cover. That's certainly a valid writing procedure, and this program is not necessarily recommending that you violate that protocol. All this tip is suggesting is that should you want to write your chapters out of sequence, that option is possible and appropriate.

The following are a few reasons why writing out of sequence might at times be beneficial:

1. It offers you creative freedom. You can write about whatever you want to write about whenever you want to write it. If you're enthused about one of your chapters, you can write it now. If you suddenly get some brilliant thoughts about a certain chapter, you can get those thoughts on paper. We writers often have to struggle to get our ideas translated to the written word, so whenever the muse visits us, it's wise to capitalize. Besides, the exuberance you have at that moment will show up in your text. Your enthusiasm will spread to your readers.

2. You can fit your chapters into your available writing time. Some chapters will be longer than others. A few will more complicated than the rest. Certain chapters may appear easier to write than others. You can adjust your writing to any of these circumstances. For instance, if you have a busy schedule at the moment and limited time to devote to writing, write one of the shorter chapters. If you have lots of time to spend at the keyboard today, maybe the longer chapter should be the

one you approach. There may be difficult chapters that seem frightening to you. Now might be a good time to attack them and get them out of the way.

3. You can complete *parts* of chapters. Each chapter has different segments. It's possible to write about any one of those segments without completing the entire chapter. Since my plan tells me what these segments are and where they belong in the chapter, I can write each piece separately. The same phenomenon will occur in your book. This may be a good way to utilize some of your writing time.

This idea works with fiction writing, too. Your story is divided into plot points and scenes. There may also be segments within those scenes. If the tale is outlined fully, you can know which segments of scenes or complete scenes you can write whenever you have the time.

CHAPTER 13

STICK TO YOUR SCHEDULE

IT'S ASTOUNDING HOW MUCH YOU'VE ACCOMPLISHED in your life. You've already achieved many feats of almost unbelievable proportions. If I asked you to do some of them today, you'd likely reply by saying, "No way. That's impossible." Yet you completed them.

What are they? I have no idea. However, you do. Consider whatever you do for a living and then look back over the years and see how much you've completed. For instance, if you're a plumber, think how many leaky faucets you've repaired or how many broken pipes you've fixed. If you're a hairdresser, picture how many washes and perms you've completed. A dry cleaner? Think of the number of shirts and trousers you've pressed. If you're a homemaker, consider the number of meals you've prepared and served. It's truly astonishing.

Now think how you managed to do all that. You've accomplished so much because you had to show up for work each day. While you were there, you were expected to produce results. So you did. In effect, you were following a schedule.

That's exactly what you must do to complete your book.

In Chapter 10 (PLAN YOUR WRITING SCHEDULE), we noted that *the schedule is the heart of my system* for starting and finishing that book you've always wanted to write. It keeps the project alive. Abandon it, and completing your book is in jeopardy.

I'm aware of this from personal experience. Many aspiring comedy writers have asked me to help them with their writing. One of my conditions for continuing to work with them was that they submit at least ten gags to me each week. That was a non-negotiable requirement. Most of them failed. "I have to paint the kitchen this week, but I'll turn in twenty gags next week." "I'm having company from out of town for awhile. I'll get back on schedule after they leave." These and excuses like them generally resulted in those writers never submitting anything again.

However, many of the students persevered in delivering the quota of gags. Several of these went on to long and profitable careers as television writers and a few graduated to films, books, and other writing avenues. These folks succeeded not because of my coaching, but because they continued to write to a schedule, a quota. They coached themselves into a writing career by continuing to produce material regularly, thereby always improving their skill. Remember, most writers insist that there are only three ways to learn to write. They are to write, to write, and to write.

Consider also a university basketball team that has solid young talent and a knowledgeable coach. Imagine if that coach announced to his players that they have the gymnasium reserved for practice for three hours each morning and another three hours after the school day ends. He tells his team, "I'll be here during those hours should you need help. You can show up on the court anytime you like and, while you're there, you can work on anything you like."

Do you think that team will be playing in the national finals in March? Probably not. In order to effectively coach a team and prepare it for competition, the coach must set rigid standards for his players. "Be here for practice at such and such a time every day—no exceptions. Skip practice without a valid excuse and you'll either be suspended from the squad or dismissed totally." Also, during practice, the coach should set standards for the team's workouts. He should work towards predetermined goals. Maybe they'll work as a team on fast breaks or coordinated defenses. He may run them through drills to build up their stamina. He may have individual players work on individual skills. Whatever the process is, it should be organized and designed to produce certain desired results.

Basically, that's what the writing schedule you devised should do for you—get you there and prod you to produce certain results. Woody Allen once joked that "seventy percent of success was showing up." There's a certain amount of wisdom in that jest. To accomplish anything worthwhile, you do have to be there. Part of the rationale for having a writing schedule is to remind you to "show up." Be there at your keyboard at certain times. Another reason for the schedule, though, is to convince you that as long as you've shown up, you might as well get something done. Those are the specific goals that you've set.

Show up and reach your pre-set, short-term goals and you'll progress steadily toward your ultimate goal—to complete your manuscript.

Remember, too, that I advised that *no one can write a book*. The best any of us can do is write one part of a book at a time. Write enough parts, piece them together intelligently, and the result is a finished book. The writing schedule guides you in selecting which part of the book you'll work on.

As important as the schedule is to your project, and even considering the amount of time you devoted to preparing it, no schedule is absolutely perfect. But that's all right. Your original plan is adjustable, and if you miscalculated, revise it. After all, this routine is supposed to get you to finish your book, not drive you to a nervous breakdown.

If you honestly discover that your plan is too demanding, relax it. Suppose you figured on writing two chapters a week, but you are having trouble keeping up with that pace. Fine. Redesign your routine so that you need to complete only three chapters every two weeks, or even one chapter a week. This, of course, will push back your proposed completion date, but that's all right, too. The idea here is to finish your book. It's not important whether you complete it in six months, nine months, or even a year.

However, should you have a contracted date and you project that you won't be able to meet it, you should advise your publisher, in a timely fashion, that you might miss the deadline and see if you can mutually negotiate a new submission date.

A key word above is "honestly." Revising your writing schedule simply to make it easier on you is risky. Keep in mind that an effective schedule should be somewhat demanding. You want to *push* yourself a little bit. That keeps up your enthusiasm for the project. It's like doing crossword puzzles. They're fun to do. However, if the puzzles are so simple that they become merely a matter of writing in the answers, then they're not fun. They're not a challenge. So, do maintain a bit of challenge, even in your revised schedule.

In fact, that may be another reason for revising your original plan—it may be too easy. Should you find that you're turning out the pages so quickly that you're zooming way ahead, perhaps you should make your schedule more demanding. You want to push your writing limits somewhat for the reasons that we spoke of above. A less than challenging schedule could become boring and could erode your enthusiasm. It could leave too much non-writing time, which can lead you to eventually forsake the project.

In other words, you don't want to get so far behind in your writing schedule that it destroys your confidence. On the other hand, you don't want to get so far ahead in your plan that you leave too much non-writing time between deadlines. That might cause you to lose interest in the project. You want to fine-tune your writing schedule so that it is, as I said in Chapter 10, demanding yet realistic, challenging yet doable.

TRACKING YOUR PROGRESS

As you complete different phases of your writing plan, record your progress. You should have a physical chart of your original plan and an up-to-date evaluation of your headway. This chart can be generated on your computer (as in the example shown in Chapter 10), or it can be a handwritten schedule that reminds you how many chapters you will complete week by week.

As you finish a chapter, note that on your schedule. Also, record how many words are in that particular chapter. This will give you not only a running tally of how many chapters you've completed, but also the total number of words in your manuscript to date.

Keeping an ongoing record tells you exactly where you are in your project. With a quick glance at your chart and a few mathematical calculations, you know how much you've accomplished and how much work you still must do.

Checking your plan periodically is a reminder that you are making steady progress, which can be encouraging. At the same time, it's prompting you to keep up the steady pace because you haven't yet completed your project.

Some business advisor once said, "If you can't measure it, you can't manage it." Starting and finishing a book is a project that requires constant oversight. Even though you're the only worker and also the boss, you still must be vigilant in husbanding this effort to completion. You are in control. Measuring your advancement along the way allows you to remain in control. If you abandon that, you run the risk of the entire project overwhelming you.

Recording your progress also shows you whether you're meeting your goals or not. In designing your schedule, you'll recall, you had a set number of chapters you would include in your book. In order to produce a reasonably sized book, you decided on a word count for each chapter.

As you maintain your records, you will know how many chapters you've completed and what the total word count is for those chapters. Dividing one into the other provides an average word count per chapter. This result tells you whether you're fulfilling the commitment you made to this book.

Just as an example, suppose you planned on writing a book of 60,000 words and you've mapped out twenty chapters in your table of contents. That means you should produce about 3,000 words in each chapter. Of course, as we discussed earlier, this doesn't mean that each of those chapters should be exactly 3,000 words in length. In fact, it makes for more enjoyable reading if the chapters vary in length. However, the average chapter should be about 3,000 words.

Let's imagine now that you've completed five representative chapters and you have produced a total of 10,000 words. The math shows that you're averaging only 2,000 words for each chapter. The resulting projection indicates that your finished manuscript will be only 40,000 words, not the 60,000 that you desired.

In order to meet your original word count, you have two choices. First, you can add a bit more substance to your writing. Try to deliver another 1000 words per chapter without overwriting. Second, you could try to add additional chapters to your manuscript. Of course, another choice is that you could resign yourself to producing a smaller manuscript.

Any of these decisions can be valid, but you recognize from your record keeping that some adjustment must be made. It's easier to handle that adjustment early in your project rather than after the manuscript is finished.

Seeing the progress you're making can also act as an incentive to continue on toward your goal. Accomplishment leads to further accomplishment. Golf is a difficult, trying game. It can be frustrating and at many times downright annoying. Yet golfers will admit to you that one excellent shot on a given day is exhilarating enough to bring them back to play the following day.

A sage once stated this idea concisely, saying, "Nothing succeeds like success." The pride of marking one chapter on your schedule "finished" inspires you to type out the next chapter so you can also mark that one "done." Then another, then another. Successfully meeting the targets you've set for yourself is often all the incentive you need to continue meeting additional goals.

Noting your continual progress makes it easier for you to eventually see "the light at the end of the tunnel." For some psychological reason, we seem to work with more resolve, more energy, and more determination when we see ourselves nearing the end of the project. Long distance runners seem to *sprint* when they come close to the finish line. Keeping track of your steady advancement brings the *finish line* of your project closer and closer. That should give you renewed determination to complete your book.

Keeping accurate records also allows you to assume more control over your entire project. Working on an entire book, from concept to completion, is a tiring task. I noted earlier that you would require time for relaxation, recuperation, rejuvenation, maybe just time away from the whole thing altogether. There would be moments when you would have to push yourself a tad further than you wanted to be pushed. There would be times, also, when you would reward yourself for work well done.

It should be fairly clear, though, that you can better decide when you need a possible R & R break if you know exactly where you are in your proposed schedule. Being constantly aware of your progress can tell you when your production is slowing down. Maybe that's when stepping away from it for awhile so that you can return to it with renewed vitality is the wisest management choice.

These decisions, in the long run, can make the entire project easier. By giving yourself the time you need to maintain your enthusiasm, you make the writing of your manuscript, from page 1 to the back cover, that much easier.

Whatever decisions you make on this project are yours. This is your book. You write it the way you want to write it and at the pace you determine. However, having a writing plan, sticking to it, and using it to keep you informed of your progress can help to make your decisions wise ones.

CHAPTER 14

REWRITING YOUR MANUSCRIPT

Congratulations! You've planned out your project, prepared a workable writing schedule, gotten to your keyboard faithfully, persevered through that schedule, and now you have a completed manuscript. That's the good news. The bad news is that your manuscript is not complete.

Oh, it's finished, but it's not *complete*. Remember, in designing your writing schedule you allowed a certain number of weeks for *preparing your manuscript for publication.* The first step in that process is to review and revise your writing. You're ready to begin that rewriting process.

There are different feelings among writers about rewriting. Some feel it's a necessary evil and try to avoid as much of it as possible. Often, this can be accomplished by doing some of your *rewriting* before you do the actual writing. That means that you plan each phase of your writing, prepare it, think it through, and then write as complete, accurate, and thorough a first draft as you possibly can. Obviously, this would cut down on the amount of rewriting you'd have to do.

Other writers feel that rewriting is the heart of the process. I've heard some writers say, "I'm not a writer; I'm a rewriter." To those writers, the initial draft is merely an outline—a road map, if you will—for the final text.

Since we began this system by admitting that it is not a writing instruction manual, the writing and rewriting process is entirely your choice. Whichever technique, or combination of techniques, works for you is fine. Write in whatever style you feel comfortable with.

However, one thing is certain—your first draft is not your final draft. It does require review and revisions. Earlier, I recommended not doing immediate rewrites. After writing a chapter, let a few days or even a few weeks go by before reviewing it. This allows you to view your writing with fresh eyes. With that advice in mind, I suggest that you complete the manuscript before beginning the rewriting process. That way, you can reread the entire book to better evaluate its content.

However, depending on how you planned your writing schedule, you may want to review portions of your manuscript as you go. Either way is fine, provided you do allow a little bit of time between the writing and the rewriting.

You want to review your manuscript in order to make it as perfect as possible before sending it for publication. There are several areas you'll want to examine before you can personally consider your text completed.

First, you want to be certain that the pages are free of mechanical flaws—typos, misspellings, incorrect punctuation, extra words included, necessary words inadvertently omitted—you know, those things that just seem to happen for whatever reason. Whether your book is an audition piece or a contracted project for a publisher, you want to eliminate as many of these errors as possible. Not only is it the professional attitude, but it's also a courtesy to the publisher and your readers. Besides, it's going to be your book, with your name on the cover, so you want to avoid embarrassing imperfections. You have no guarantee that the publisher's staff will find and correct all of them.

Second, you want to assure yourself that the text is free of "logic" flaws. Duplication may sneak into your manuscript. Is the anecdote you recount on page 78 the same as the one you told earlier on page 23? Or, even worse, is the anecdote you relate on page 78, the same as the one you told on page 23… except with different names and places? Contradictions are another common flaw. If you make a statement in Chapter 2, you don't want to discover that you offer a completely opposite opinion in Chapter 14. As I mentioned earlier, in my book on comedy writing I cited an example of a book where the author declared authoritatively on page 1 that comedy writing could neither be taught nor learned. Then on page 3 the author thanked "The man who taught me everything I know about comedy writing."

Are the illustrations and examples you include valid and verifiable? You don't want to retell stories that have been proven to be false. You don't want to cite mythical tales as if they were true, unless you admit that even though they're apocryphal, they are helpful in emphasizing a certain point.

You want your reasoning and your reporting to be credible. Your recommendations should be consistent. If you attribute a witty quote to Mark Twain, you should be certain that Mark Twain said it—not Woody Allen.

Third, surely you want your book to be well-written. You want to know that your ideas in each chapter flow from one point to the next in a logical progression. You want your sentences to be well-constructed, your verbs to be powerful, your adjectives and adverbs to be not only appropriate, but also serve a purpose in the text. You want to eliminate awkward sounding sentences. You want a book that reads *easily*.

Fourth, you want your text to say what you intended it to say. You had a basic purpose in writing this book. Does the finished first draft convey your thoughts? Have you explained everything fully to your readers? Are your examples appropriate and to the point? Do they really illustrate the concept you're trying explain? Is it possible that you've over-explained some of your thoughts? Maybe you've used too many examples and confused the account? Have you overloaded the concept with too many supporting quotes or analogies?

REVIEWING AND REVISING YOUR MANUSCRIPT

With these goals in mind, here are a few suggestions for reviewing your text:

First, reread the entire book just to get a feel for the overall effect. In other words, don't worry about correcting typos, or rewriting sentences or paragraphs. Try to force yourself to read the piece from beginning to end without being distracted by making notes and rewriting on the fly. This should give you either a satisfied feeling that your book has accomplished what you wanted it to accomplish, or it should leave you with that uneasy belief that portions of it need more work. Probably, it will result in a combination of both. Some chapters are brilliant; others are wanting.

It doesn't really matter which happens, so long as you have a *feel* for your manuscript.

Second, go through the manuscript noting all those typos and flaws that pop out at you. At this point, though, you're not really rewriting the text; you're simply eliminating mechanical flaws. This is really proofreading, rather than rewriting. Nevertheless, it's a necessary task in order to turn in a flawless manuscript. Correcting typos should be your major concern at this point. Fretting too much about other concerns may distract you from this simple, but essential task.

Nevertheless, as you read through the pages, you will spot places where you'd like to rearrange paragraphs or restructure sentences. You might find some stories that you think are duplicates. If so, you might quickly note your concern in the margin and highlight that with a question mark. You'll come back to these in a later session.

Once you've got the typos marked and edited, you can go into the computer and make the changes. In this case, it may be easier to work chapter by chapter rather than going through the entire text. However, again, that's your choice.

Third, go through your manuscript either from start to finish or chapter by chapter and do your style rewriting. Change the sentence structure where needed, enliven your vocabulary, be more concise in your phrasing. In other words, do whatever it takes for you to write the book with a polished, professional technique.

At the same time, you can now attack those items you questioned earlier in your rewriting. You remember—those items you earlier noted with a question mark in the margin. Rewrite them so that you can be confident now that those are written the way you want them written.

Also, check the logic of your arguments. Do they make sense? Are your explanations and illustrations clear and appropriate? Have you eliminated all duplications?

Fourth, there may be areas where you're not satisfied that you've explained your concepts correctly or clearly enough. You know what you intended to say, but as you've read through your manuscript, you may decide that you could manage to say it better.. This may require extensive rewrites in certain portions of your text. Now is your chance to make sure that you've said all the things that you set out to say when you began this project way back when.

Your manuscript is now complete (well, almost complete), so this is a good opportunity to give it one more quick run-through, just as a final check. When you're satisfied that you've written a worthwhile book, you're ready to prepare it for publication.

CHAPTER 15

PREPARING YOUR MANUSCRIPT
FOR PUBLICATION

YOUR TEXT IS COMPLETED. It's been reviewed, rewritten, polished, checked and rechecked. It's ready to go. However, if you open up a book—any book—you'll see that there is more in that book than the body of text for that particular volume. For example, I've picked two books at random.

The first began with four pages of praise for the book from experts in this particular field. The copyright information page followed that. The dedication page was next. Then there was the title page, followed by the table of contents. The prologue came next, followed by the chapters. This book also had an epilogue and an addendum. And there was also a promotional page listing a website for additional information on subjects related to the book, available DVDs, and a listing of other books by this author. It also had the author's contact information.

There were also five pages of acknowledgments, and then a series of endnotes listing resources that were cited in each chapter of the book. Finally, there was a complete index and a two-page biography of the author. Following that, though, there was also a page listing other books available from this particular publishing house. Of course, there was also the text on the back cover and a brief description of the book on the inside front flap and an author biography on the inside back flap.

That's a lot of pages, aside from the actual text of the book.

The second book I selected at random began with two pages of praise for the author and the book, quoting notable people in the field. Then there was the copyright page, the title page, the table of contents, and a page of acknowledgments from the author.

Next was an introduction written by the author, followed by the prologue. Following that was the text of the book, running from chapter 1 through chapter 13. After that were several pages of "resources" and then the appendices (which were mostly samples of documents discussed in the book). The index completed the book. Again, of course, there was text on the back cover, which included a biography of the author.

Some of this additional material, such as the table of contents, should absolutely be submitted with your manuscript; however, you should strongly consider supplying other additional information to your publisher. Let's go through these elements to make sure that you are including everything with your submission that you would like to see in the published copy of your book.

First let's consider **praise** for your book. I like to call these "blurbs," although "endorsements" may be a more technical and correct term. These are those short paragraphs that strongly recommend either the contents of this book or you as the author. They should come from recognized and notable people in the field you're writing about; however, there are exceptions to that. In this book you're presently reading, for instance, I included in my manuscript several blurbs from students who have taken my classes. With my allegorical novel, *Breakfasts with Archangel Shecky*, I played with the "blurb" concept whimsically. The novel is about a person who claims to be a guardian angel. So, rather than get endorsements from associates of mine in the comedy writing profession, I manufactured endorsements from people who would know a guardian angel. Here is an example from that book's back cover:

> "I've worked with a lot of hopeless cases in my career. Archangel Shecky has always been one of my favorites. His wisdom can help many people who feel their careers are hopeless."
> —*St. Jude, Patron of Lost Causes*

Worthwhile endorsements can be a helpful marketing tool for both yourself and your publisher, so endeavor to obtain some and submit them with your text. And don't be afraid to "shoot for the sky." Well-known people are often more willing than you might think to lend a blurb.

You can include praise you've gathered either at the beginning or at the end of your manuscript. Keep in mind that the publishing staff will decide precisely where the items should be placed in the final book. And, should the publisher decide not to include them in the book itself, they may still serve a useful purpose in other ways. For example, the publishing company might feature blurbs as part of the advance promotion for the book.

If you have **acknowledgments** you want to include in your book, you should include these as part of your submission. Acknowledgments are those pages from the author thanking many of the people who helped in writing or publishing the book. They often include editors, publishing staff, agents, family, advisors, and the like. You'll notice in the books that I used as examples, one had the acknowledgments up front, the other at the end. That choice is yours. You can place the copy for this item wherever you would like to see it in your published book. Understand, though, that the publishers may choose to move it.

You should include a **title page** for your submitted manuscript. The title page simply lists the title of the book, the subtitle (if you have one), and your name as the author. The publisher will surely redesign the page, but including it adds a professional flair to your submission.

The **copyright page**, you can ignore. That will be supplied by the publisher when the book is printed.

A **dedication page** is not an essential part of your book, but I suggest you include one. I've said all along that starting and completing a book is a formidable task. It requires devotion, effort, and perseverance. With this completed text, you've earned the right to dedicate the book to whomever you want. Why not include that page in your submission?

The **table of contents** is a critical element that lists the various components of the book: the acknowledgments, the introduction, the prologue, whatever front material or back material you have, and a listing of the chapters, along with the page numbers for each. Your table of contents will be a helpful common reference point with the editor and publisher. These page numbers, of course, will be for your typewritten manuscript. Although you should be sure to double-check your page number references for correctness, note that the publisher will take care of listing the final page numbers for the finished volume.

Consider getting creative with your table of contents. Many people glance through the table of contents when considering whether to buy a book or not. When Amazon.com invites people to "search inside this book," it always includes the contents page as part of that search. If you can make yours more enticing and appealing, go ahead and do it.

As examples, in one of my books the publisher added a brief synopsis of each chapter in the contents, and they noted a few of the elements that would be covered in each chapter. Also, some authors like to begin each chapter with a quote that applies; listing this quote as a sort of subtitle for each chapter heading might also garner additional interest. If you have other creative ideas, include them so the publisher can see and evaluate them. Again, this is your book, and you write it your way. However, be prepared for the editor or the publisher changing or deleting your additions. You'll notice those when you get your proof copies to review. You can negotiate with the publisher then, if you choose to do so.

A **foreword** is not required. This piece normally is located at the beginning of the book and is written by someone other than the author. It usually tells a bit about the book and how the foreword writer is connected to the book's author. If you can find someone of stature to supply a foreword, it's a big boost to your book. It adds some credibility to your writing, and it makes for a nice line on the front cover—"with foreword by *somebody important.*" The foreword should be signed by the writer and there should be some sort of verification offered to the publisher that this person actually agreed to supply this piece.

Supplying a **preface**, **introduction**, **prologue**, or any other bit of writing that you feel is essential to your message, but precedes Chapter 1, is entirely up to you. None of these are strictly required, and none of them will really be missed if they're not included. However, if you, as the author, feel that you want such a piece in your volume, it's your responsibility to add it to the manuscript.

After the front matter, we finally get to Chapter 1 and continue sequentially through to the final chapter.

If you have a list of resources, appendices, endnotes, or other back matter, include that as part of your manuscript.

Most books devote a page, a portion of the inside back flap, or the back cover to the author's biography. Sometimes, the publishers will generate this copy, or they may ask you to write it. However, if you want to be sure that it's included and you feel confident in supplying your own biography, write it and include it with your manuscript submission. The publisher then has the option of using it as is, or of rewriting it. Again, you'll get a chance to review it with your proof copies. Anything you want included, deleted, or changed, you can note and discuss with the publisher.

Should you include a **promotional page**? This is a page that lists other items you have available—other books, CDs, DVDs, classes or seminars you host, or clubs that you promote. It can also include your website and other contact information you want to make available to readers of this book. If you have such material to promote, write up a page and include it as part of your manuscript submission package. This at least serves notice to the publisher that you would like to include such a page.

One publisher has told me that if the material is directly related to the subject matter of the book, it could very well enhance the appeal of the book. If it is simply a sales pitch for other unrelated items, the publisher may opt not to make it a part of the published book.

Depending on the nature of your book, an **index** may be necessary. This is not the time to be concerned with that process, though. First of all, any page numbers you include will most likely change in the publishing process. If the indexing is contractually your obligation, the publisher will probably contact you later when the final pages are determined. You can do the work or have it done at that time. Usually, the publisher will hire this task out. Whatever the agreement is, it should be handled later.

SUBMITTING YOUR MANUSCRIPT

Now, let's discuss the logistics of submitting your manuscript. I advise that you create a master computer file that includes your entire book, complete with all front and back material. Repaginate it, beginning with page 1 on to the end of the manuscript. Publishers have told me that the page numbering of the manuscript is not that important because it has little relation to the book once it is laid out by the book's designer. Nevertheless, as we noted earlier, the manuscript pages should be numbered so that in discussions with the editor or the publisher, you'll both have a common reference point. Be wary, though, that in repaginating, any references you have in your manuscript to page numbers might change. You should check for any such references before submitting your book.

Should you have pictures or graphic elements that are tied to a particular part of your manuscript, you should flag this in the manuscript with a note to the editor. That note should clearly state where the specific element should be located in relationship to the text.

Most publishers prefer Microsoft Word. Avoid getting too fancy in the presentation of the text. Times New Roman, 12 pt. is the accepted font. Using formatting, such as italics and bold fonts, is acceptable. If you have certain portions of your text where a different font is absolutely essential, then use a different font. However, the book designer may change that to another type of formatting.

Publishers say that it's a waste of time for the author to spend too much time worrying about layout and positioning of elements, since the book will be redesigned before publication anyway.

It's recommended that you also submit a hard copy of your manuscript along with the computer disc. Publishers tell me that the printed copy is still useful, even in today's magical digital age, in part because many editors still prefer to do their work by putting pen to paper.

The hard copy should be submitted unbound, which makes it easier for the publisher to photocopy, should they need to give different sections of the book to different readers or editors.

> Different publishers may have different demands for receiving submissions. It's only common sense to give them the manuscript in whichever form they prefer. How do you know what they would like?
>
> If you have a contract, those logistics should be listed there. If you are submitting on spec, you could:
>
> - Check the publisher's requests in a writer's market list.
> - Check the publisher's website for any submission guides.
> - Write to the publisher, requesting any written information on submitting material.
> - Call the publishing office and ask how manuscripts should be submitted.

Now, before you send it off, give your entire submission package another inspection.

First, make sure you have included all of the elements you want to include. Did you remember to write and include a dedication page? Have you written any acknowledgments you wanted to make? Is the table of contents complete with the manuscript page numbers? Are those numbers correct? Here's one that I often overlook: Are the chapter headings listed in the table of contents in agreement with the chapter headings in the text?

Second, go through the entire manuscript page by page. Are the pages in the correct order? Are all of the pages "present and accounted for?" It's embarrassing to turn in a hard copy and discover that pages 79 through 85 are missing. Should they be there? If not, shouldn't whatever page follows page 79 be page 80, and not page 86? You get the idea.

Third, be sure that your chapters are in sequential order, too. You may have the correct page numbers in the proper sequence, but discover that entire chapters are out of sequence.

Fourth, be sure that any references to page numbers in the text are correct. Remember, you repaginated the text and those references might now be inaccurate.

It only takes a brief time to go through this final check, but it's well worth it in reassurance value. Errors are not only time-consuming for both you and the publisher, but they also show a sign of laziness or carelessness. If you're to begin an association with an editor and a publisher, it's worth a little extra time and effort to get things started well, and professionally.

You'll have an opportunity is to review the proof copies that the publisher sends you and to make any last minute adjustments and corrections. Then, just sit back and wait for your "author's copies" to arrive in the mail, delight in the look and feel of the published book, and sign a few for friends.

It's a great feeling, isn't it?

CHAPTER 16

YOU'RE DONE!

THAT'S IT. YOU'VE FINALLY REACHED THAT POINT that I'm sure you doubted at times along the way that you would ever reach. The book is written, finished, completed. You're done.

But are you really done?

How about that other book you've been wanting to write?

Maybe you're just beginning.

SOME SUPPORT MIGHT HELP

ONE ADVANTAGE OF WRITING IS THAT it's a solitary chore. It's just you, your thoughts, and your keyboard. One disadvantage of writing is that it's a solitary chore. It's just you, your thoughts, and your keyboard. These two concepts may not be as contradictory as they first appear. Consider a dad with young children. It's often a delight for him to roll around the floor with the kids, tickling, wrestling, and laughing with them. It's heavenly. Yet after a particularly harrowing day at the office and a stressful ride home on the crowded highways, he might simply want to slip off his necktie and shoes, relax in his easy chair, and maybe enjoy a cocktail before dinner. Wrestling with the kids on the floor is not particularly welcome to him then.

Writing can be similar. When you prefer solitude and when you prefer camaraderie is determined by how you feel and what you need at each specific moment. Which is preferred? Which is the ideal? Neither one is. It's most likely a combination of both, depending on what your writing needs are.

I won't delve into the pros and cons of writing alone, which are fairly obvious. Most of your writing will probably be done alone, and, if you're like most writers, you'll usually be most productive when you're working by yourself.

But are there times when it's advisable to mingle, fraternize, socialize and hang around with other writers? Absolutely! In fact, there may be times when it's almost necessary for you in order to finish your manuscript. Let me give you some reasons why this is so:

1. **Socializing**

   Sure, it's nice when you're working to be free from distractions and the input of others. However, it can also be lonely. Occasionally, it's comforting to *schmooze*—to join others in the profession and talk about the book that you're writing alone or to listen to others talk about the books that they're writing alone. Sometimes it's refreshing to break out of solitary confinement and mingle with the other prisoners of the writing addiction.

2. **Change of Pace**

   I mentioned many times that starting and completing a book is not easy. It's challenging and it requires organization, discipline, and dedication. It also demands considerable time at the keyboard, which can be wearying. So it's rejuvenating to escape from that occasionally. Go to a meeting, take a class, attend a seminar. Even at a seminar, you don't necessarily have to take the courses or attend the lectures. It's enjoyable and a welcome distraction simply to attend the luncheons, dinners, and cocktail parties. You're working hard on your book, so you're entitled to a "vacation" now and then.

3. **Support**

   The purpose of writers' clubs and writers' seminars is to educate, but also to both accept and offer support, as needed, to other people in the profession. Getting some assistance from other writers may be just what you need to sustain the momentum required to complete your book. Thomas Mann once said, "A writer is someone for whom writing is more difficult than it is for other people." We often need encouragement; we need reinforcement. Who better to get those from than other writers?

   There will be times in the writing of your book that you'll feel dejected, perhaps ready to quit. The support of the other members of writing clubs can often convince you to continue working. Richard Bach said, "A professional writer is an amateur who didn't quit." Sometimes we need a kick in the pants from our colleagues to convince us to be an amateur *who doesn't quit.*

4. **An Opportunity to Gather General Information about Writing**

   Writing clubs provide an almost unlimited supply of writing information. They offer newsletters, special interest groups within the club, and suggest educational opportunities and worthwhile how-to books on writing and publishing. Many clubs invite guest speakers who are experts in different facets of publishing. Sitting and listening to them is a great education. At seminars and conventions, you converse with many people in the industry: publishers, editors, agents, fellow writers. A sharp listener can learn much about the writing life and the publishing industry.

One writer came to our comedy writing convention with a plan. He was fairly successful at selling comedy locally, but he wanted to convert that to a more lucrative, widespread career. He questioned everyone about how he might accomplish that. He asked the faculty members. He asked the other attendees. He probably even questioned the hotel bartender about it once or twice, too.

Obviously, he gathered many opinions and countless suggestions. He took this information home, organized it, analyzed it, and most importantly, applied it. Within six months he was writing comedy for at least three of the most prominent comics on the national scene. Within one year, he was writing for a major television show. He has enjoyed a non-stop successful television career since then.

5. Creative Input

Regardless of the type of book you're presently working on, you will come across certain areas where you're stymied. You're either not sure what you want to say or you can't find the optimum way of saying it. Often, you'll need some help in solving your creative problem, and writers' clubs can supply that help.

Here are two ways they can assist you:

- **Formal help:** Writers clubs will often offer critiques of your writing. You'll read part of your book and other members will offer suggestions. They can also read what you've written and offer formal reviews. In open discussions, you might mention your writing problem and have the other members offer possible suggestions. Also, at many gatherings, the professionals—publishers, agents, and editors—may offer to read your submissions and present constructive suggestions.
- **Informal help:** In simple conversation with other members of the writing club, you may ask for and receive help in solving your dilemma. In some cases, critiques and suggestions that are formally offered to other writers may also provide the advice you need with your specific writing roadblock.

6. **Develop Valuable Professional Writing Contacts**

At writers' club meetings, conventions, seminars, and classes, you will meet and socialize with publishers, agents, editors, publicists, and other writers. Often, these relationships lead to career benefits.

This happened to me several times in my career. At several weekend writing seminars that I attended, I developed a friendship with a magazine editor. When we went to dinner one evening at one of the conventions, he mentioned that he felt that humor could contribute considerably to a periodical's popularity and readership. I asked if I he would like me to write a few humorous articles for his consideration. He did...and I did. He liked the audition pieces I submitted and his magazine hired me as a monthly humor columnist—an association that continued for about nine years. This magazine also formed a book division which published eight of my books.

Good things can happen when you form solid professional contacts.

7. **You May Become a Leader in the Organization and Benefit from that Experience**

You might become active in your local writing organization by becoming an officer, chairing one of the special interest groups, or giving occasional lectures or presentations to the club. Each of these can be helpful to you.

You don't have to be an expert or a recognized authority to accomplish any of these goals. A writers' club is formed so that the writers, both the accomplished and the aspiring, can assist one another. So, you're as qualified to run for office, chair a group, or make a presentation as any of the other members.

8. **Renew Enthusiasm**

The whole experience of getting out of your private office and associating with others in the writing and publishing profession can revitalize your enthusiasm for your book project.

As a kid, I used to go to my big brother's high school football games each Sunday during the season. The games were fun and exciting, regardless of whether our team won or lost. But each time I came home from the stadium, I was eager to go in, change into play clothes, and go out and play a game of two-hand touch football. Watching his games got me enthused about playing football.

The same can happen to you as a writer. Completing a book is a challenge—we've said that before. Anything that can keep your enthusiasm for that project alive is worth exploring. Getting into the social aspects of writing society may very well serve that purpose.

The writing community can indeed be helpful to you in starting and completing your book. However, there are a few caveats too.

The first caution is to *listen attentively, but selectively.* Remember that this is *your* book. The ideas in the book are *your* ideas. *You* make all the final decisions, in *your* own mind and heart, on what goes into your manuscript. *You* make those decisions regardless of whether your writing comrades agree with them or not.

The next caveat is to *be wary of criticism.* Actually, you should be wary not so much of the criticism as of your reaction to it. When you expose yourself and your writing project to the opinions of others, you must be willing to accept that some of those opinions may be negative. Try to listen to all suggestions with an open mind and without prejudice. Refer back to the first caution above and remember that you don't have to apply any of those suggestions if you don't feel they help your book.

However, even though you may not accept the suggestions, you may still allow the negativity to affect you and your writing. Try not to take any of it personally, and, above all, don't allow it to deter you from your main goal—completing your book.

The third caution is to *keep your own drive and initiative active despite the promises of others.* At these gatherings, as we discussed, you may make some pretty impressive professional contacts. Well-meaning people may offer to do this or that for you. It's wise to take advantage of these proposals. They can often be quite helpful. However—and this is the big caveat—don't surrender your own activity on your own behalf to these promises. Continue to work on your own to further your career.

It's tempting to turn your success over to others, but it's not wise. In my comedy writing career, I've met many aspiring writers who hadn't yet made a sale, who said, "I landed an agent. I know I'm going to be working in television soon." I would respond, "No, it doesn't necessarily mean that. You haven't sold anything yet. Having an agent could simply mean that now there are two of you who can't find you work."

That may sound unusually cruel, but it's not meant to be. I would go on to explain to these writers that even though they now had an agent, which could turn out to be a good thing, they still had to devote much of their own time and effort to furthering their career.

The same caution applies to any wonderful offers you may receive from colleagues in the publishing trade. Accept whatever help others can give you, but don't rely on it to the exclusion of your own hard work toward your goals.

So, do enjoy the advantages of socializing with fellow writers and hobnobbing with the publishing elite, but remember you still have a book to complete. To do that, you must get back to the solitude of your private writing world. It's time to return to your creativity, your thoughts, your keyboard, and your future readers.

ABOUT THE AUTHOR

GENE PERRET has earned his living as a professional writer since 1964. He began writing comedy material for nightclub performers such as Phyllis Diller and Slappy White. That led to a career as a television writer and producer for such shows as *The Carol Burnett Show, Laugh-In, The New Bill Cosby Show, All in the Family, Three's Company, Welcome Back, Kotter, The Tim Conway Show,* and others. He was on Bob Hope's writing staff for 28 years, the last dozen of those acting as Hope's head-writer. He has been awarded 3 Emmys and one Writer's Guild Award.

Gene has written about 40 books—how-to volumes on writing, collections of humor, and one allegorical novel. He has also contributed articles to magazines such as *Reader's Digest, McCall's, Ladies' Home Journal, Parenting, Toastmaster,* and others. He wrote a monthly humor column called "Wit Stop" for over nine years for *Arizona Highways.*

Today he plays golf, writes special material for performers, and teaches writing courses in his hometown and via e-mail. Be sure to check Gene Perret's website, **www.ComedyWritersRoom.com**, to order his books and to learn more about the e-mail courses he teaches—with personal feedback and critiques—on various aspects of humor writing.

Following are other books by Gene Perret on the writing profession:

Become a Richer Writer (Shift Your Writing Career into High Gear)
(Jester Press, 1996, $14.95)
All writers hit a career slump (or a suppose career slump) at some time or another. This book offers various remedies for getting a stalled career moving again. Whether the problem is your approach to writing, your writing, or the marketing of your product, this volume offers relief.

Damn! That's Funny (Writing Humor You Can Sell)
(Quill Driver Books,2005, $14.95)
This is a book on writing humorous magazine articles. It includes tips on how and where to get ideas for humor, and how to market what you write. It also lists various styles of humorous articles and offers advice on writing each style.

The New Comedy Writing Step by Step
(Quill Driver Books, 2007, $14.95)
This is an updated version of *Comedy Writing Step by Step* that was originally published in 1982 and has been the *bible* for comedians and comedy writers ever since. The book is a thorough how-to manual that not only encourages and inspires would be writers, but also guides them step by step through the comedy writing process—from the blank pages to the completed manuscript.

Breakfasts with Archangel Shecky (and His Infallible, Irrefutable, Unassailable, One-Size-Fits-All Secrets of Success)
(Quill Driver Books, 2009, $19.95)
This is a fictional story of a young Philadelphian who is struggling to become a recognized standup comedian. Circumstances begin to change for the better when he meets a stranger who calls himself "Archangel Shecky" and claims to be the comic's Guardian Angel.

This angel loves to drink scotch and eat all of the foods that Philly is famous for—cheese steaks, hoagies, soft pretzels, and such. However, he hates to—and refuses to—pick up any bar tabs or restaurant checks.

Yet he offers solid advice on comedy—not just on comedy, though. Also on how to achieve whatever you want in any profession.

Is "Shecky" angelic or is he a dead beat? Is his wisdom valid or simply a ploy to get free scotch? All of these questions are resolved in *Breakfasts with Archangel Shecky.*

Practical books for the working writer from Quill Driver Books

$14.95 ($19.95 *Canada*)

The New Comedy Writing Step by Step

A Writer's Digest Book Club Selection!
—by Emmy Award-winning writer Gene Perret

Three-time Emmy-award winner Gene Perret's Comedy Writing Step by Step has been the manual for humor writers for 24 years. With this, his first update, Perret offers readers a treasure trove of guidelines and suggestions covering a broad range of comedy writing situations, along with many all-important insights into the selling of one's work.

❝ Gene Perret is the world's top authority on comedy writing ... thinking ... and presentation. ❞
—Phyllis Diller

$14.95 ($19.95 *Canada*)

Emotional Structure
Creating the Story Beneath the Plot
—by Emmy and Peabody Award-winning producer and writer Peter Dunne

Using his three decades of experience writing and producing scrips ("Dallas," "Melrose Place," "CSI," and others), Peter Dunne takes the reader through a step-by-step process of creating a script whose emotional composition rings true and whose arrangement of complex character conflicts for the story's ultimate passion. Designed for aspiring as well as experienced writers, *Emotional Structure* teaches the nuts and bolts of key craft issues such as plot structure, conflict and crisis, scene construction, and dialogue.

❝ The first book every aspiring writer should read. ❞
—Chip Chalmers, Filmmaker in Residence, Florida State University

$14.95 ($19.95 *Canada*)

Damn! Why Didn't I Write That?
How Ordinary People Are Raking In $100,000 or More Writing Nonfiction Books & How You Can Too!
—by Marc McCutcheon, former literary agent and bestselling author

More nonfiction books are breaking the 100,000-copy sales barrier than ever before. Amateur writers, housewives, and even high school dropouts have cashed in with astonishingly simple bestsellers. This newly updated guide will show you how you can get in on the action by identifying lucrative publishing niches and filling them, not once, not twice, but year after year.

❝ This book has everything you need to turn your ideas into cash. ❞
—Book-of-the-Month Club

Available from bookstores, online bookstores, and QuillDriverBooks.com, or by calling toll-free 1-800-345-4447.

New Books for Writers
from Quill Driver Books

$14.95 ($16.95 *Canada*)

101 Best Sex Scenes Ever Written
An Erotic Romp Through Literature for Writers and Readers
—by Barnaby Conrad

For writers and readers, no part of a story is more exciting — or more potentially embarrassing — than what William F. Buckley called "the obligatory sex scene." Bestselling author Barnaby Conrad (*Matador* and *The Second Life of John Wilkes Booth*) puts his formidable critical powers to work analyzing what makes a sex scene genuine literature, and he provides a feast of unsurpassed examples from the world's greatest writers. Writers will learn how to write sex scenes with authenticity, credibility, and a genuine feeling for the motives, actions, and emotions of real living human beings.

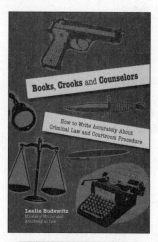

$14.95 ($16.95 *Canada*)

Books, Crooks and Counselors
How to Write Accurately About Criminal Law and Courtroom Procedure
—by Leslie Budewitz, mystery writer and attorney at law

Whether you write murder mysteries, suspense thrillers, or courtroom dramas, you want to get it right when using legal concepts and terminology or depicting courtroom procedure. *Books, Crooks and Counselors* is an easy-to-use, practical, and reliable guidebook that shows writers how to use the law to create fiction that is accurate, true-to-life, and crackling with real-world tension and conflict. Leslie Budewitz, a practicing lawyer (and mystery writer) with over 25 years of courtroom experience, will teach you the facts of legal procedure, what lawyers and judges really think about the law, and authentic courtroom dialogue.

Available from bookstores, online bookstores, and
QuillDriverBooks.com, or by calling toll-free 1-800-345-4447.

Accurate answers from a real shrink ... a unique writer's reference!

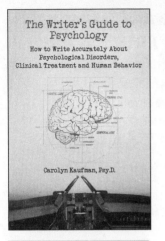

The Writer's Guide to
Psychology

How to Write Accurately About
Psychological Disorders,
Clinical Treatment and Human Behavior

Carolyn Kaufman, Psy.D.

$14.95 ($16.95 *Canada*)

The Writer's Guide to Psychology
How to Write Accurately About Psychological Disorders, Clinical Treatment and Human Behavior
—*by Carolyn Kaufman, Psy.D.*

Writers frequently write about mental illness and psychological motivations, but all too often they use terms and concepts that are clichéd, outmoded or just plain wrong.

Written by a clinical psychologist who is also a professional writer and writing coach, *The Writer's Guide to Psychology* is an authoritative, accessible, fun, and easy-to-use reference to psychological disorders, diagnosis, treatments, psychotherapists' work and what really makes psychopathic villains tick.

The only reference book on psychology designed specifically for writers, *The Writer's Guide to Psychology* presents specific writing dos and don'ts to avoid the psychobabble clichés and misunderstandings frequently seen in popular writing. The book's extensive sidebars include "Don't Let This Happen to You!" boxes that humorously expose mortifying mistakes in fiction, film and TV ... and teach readers how to get it right in their own writing.

The Writer's Guide to Psychology is a unique combination of accurate psychology, myth-busting information and practical guidance that belongs on every writer's reference shelf.

DON'T LET THIS HAPPEN TO YOU!

In *New Moon*, the follow-up to Stephenie Meyer's bestselling novel *Twilight*, the author repeatedly confuses hallucinations with delusions, using the two words interchangeably. "I was addicted to the sound of my delusions," the heroine, Bella, says. This is impossible, since delusions are ideas or beliefs. Hearing voices and seeing things both fall into the category of hallucinations.

❝ This book should be in every writer's professional library and every clinician's, too — whether writers or not!❞
—New York Journal of Books

Available from bookstores, online bookstores, and
QuillDriverBooks.com, or by calling toll-free 1-800-345-4447.